Shut Up and Ski

Wipeouts, shootouts and blowouts on the trail to the Olympic dream.

Edie Thys Morgan

Foreword/Disclaimer

If you knew me back in the day,
read this first!

This is a work of fiction, derived from my experiences competing as an athlete on the US Ski Team and the US Olympic Team. People often ask why I chose to fictionalize the story, and here's the answer. I originally intended this to be a work of nonfiction. However, the story involved so many main and supporting characters that it would have been virtually impossible for anyone who wasn't along for the ride to keep track of them all. And yet, all of the characters, their roles and the scenes they inhabited were key to telling the story. My solution was to condense many characters into fewer characters. In doing so fiction became the vehicle.

The side bonus of fictionalizing was the freedom to draw from some characters and scenes that did not fit precisely within the one-year time frame of this book. The side hazard of fictionalizing is that readers with any knowledge of the events will inevitably try to match each character with a real person. For anyone trying to do so the discrepancies may drive you nuts.

Everything in these pages happened to real people, but the main characters portrayed here are composites of many people—coaches, athletes and supporters from my era, and from the eras before and since. Once all these people and their dominant traits became distilled into purely fictionalized forms, each character then expanded to play as big a role as possible.

Take, for example, "Ken" and "Lucy." Ken is certainly none of the incredibly supportive coaches battling in the trenches with us that year. Rather, he is the messenger for the policies and philosophies that drove the US Ski Team culture during that era. And Lucy, rather than one person, represents the athletes—on US Ski Teams and on teams of all kinds throughout history—who find a way to thrive even in the least hospitable environments.

Much of the dialog was created or recreated but my goal was to portray the emotions and sentiments of the moment accurately. As for the European competitors, I left their real names and accomplishments well enough alone. All conversations and interactions with them are as and when they actually happened.

Some of the incidents happened earlier or later than stated in this book, but they all happened. The crashes are all real—I couldn't fake those. And the crushes were crushingly real. Our Murphy's Law year of extraordinarily bad luck also revealed extraordinary character, forged lifelong friendships, and proved to me that even in outcomes that appear to be failures, there is honor.

I hope you enjoy the story, whether it is a trip back in time, or a glimpse into the backstage reality of World Class sports. Most of all, I hope this reminds aspiring athletes, and those who care about them, that the reward is in the journey.

Prologue

Jackson Hole, WY, a cold day in February, 1976

"You're going down, Jamie. This time, you're going down!" I'm not really sure what possessed me to say those words to myself, or to believe them, but they were about to change my life. My older brother Jamie was ahead of me, making high speed turns down the final steep slope of Jackson Hole's main run, the Gros Ventre. We'd been doing this all week, so I knew the routine. That last run of each day, through silent agreement, was our speed run.

We'd start at the top of the mountain, in air that sparkled with floating crystals, air so cold and crisp that it froze the hairs in your nostrils if you inhaled through an uncovered nose. The snow, sucked dry from so many sub-zero winter nights, squeaked like Styrofoam underneath our skis. From where we perched atop the expanse of Rendezvous Bowl, a frozen white ocean that rolled over the horizon, the finish lay 4,139 vertical feet below us. No other ski area in America is that steep, that relentless, which is exactly why my Dad brought us here every year, and why we couldn't get enough of it.

After a day of exploring the mountain, searching for rock outcroppings to launch ourselves off, and fluffy powder snow stashed in the mountain's wooded folds, my brother and I crammed into the tram for one last trip to the summit. Just short of the top station, the tram swayed in the gusty wind, dangling from its cable over the fearsome Corbett's Couloir. Whenever I had a spot by the window I stared into the abyss, imagining the day I'd ski it, probably behind Jamie. You had to be really good or really crazy to jump into Corbett's. Jamie was both.

His need for speed had increased ever since we'd watched Franz Klammer win the 1976 Olympic Downhill race a week earlier. That night, my sisters and brother and I had clustered in the living room in our pajamas to watch ABC's Olympic broadcast from Innsbruck, Austria. We leaned in so close to the TV screen that our faces were bathed in its bluish light, and watched as Klammer, the young Austrian, exploded out of a mountaintop start shack framed by a bright blue sky. He poled madly down the course and, with every new camera angle, he hurtled into view in an unlikely part of the frame—always too wide or too low—his skis bouncing and clattering like pick-up sticks carelessly thrown down. The commentator, Bob Beattie, screamed so excitedly that his voice started cracking as Klammer sped into the shadows where the race course became nothing but a gray-white ribbon, and his body a mere streak of yellow careening down it, like a tiny action figure being tossed to its demise. Miraculously he willed himself upright every time his body launched into the air, and even his recovery moves looked predetermined, like water gushing downhill, splitting and jetting over obstacles but always rejoining along its course. As we watched Klammer cross the finish line to victory, we were all awestruck. But only one of us thought he'd actually seen God.

Klammer's newest disciple always picked the most direct route down Jackson Hole for our final run. I followed Jamie as closely as I could, and my Dad trailed somewhere in the distance. Long before I was old enough to ponder the question of when life begins, I knew from Dad that life begins when you learn how to ski. Because I was the littlest in my family to learn to ski (at two years of age), and thereby to achieve personhood, his name for me was "Little Person." At nine years of age, in my seventh year of personhood, I still had neither the mass nor the nerve to get in front of Jamie. But my lifetime thus far, spent perpetually in pursuit of three older siblings, had taught me a thing or two about physics. First, less weight means less momentum. My only chance at keeping up was to cut corners and scramble into Jamie's slipstream. Even that didn't work on the flat cat-track sections of the hill where he pulled away easily. Less mass also meant less air resistance, so I made myself as small as possible to keep in range.

Finally, when common sense yielded to poor judgment and pride, as it often did, I depended on the knowledge that the shortest distance between two points is a straight line. That must be what prompted the inner voice that suddenly took command. Even though the hill ahead continued to drop steeply around a blind corner, I pointed my skis straight down the mountain.

"I don't care if I'm only 75 pounds," the voice insisted. "I don't care if these puny skis aren't designed to withstand half this speed. I don't care that I have no idea what to do once I pass you. You are going down, Jamie!"

With that, I assumed what would become my most

familiar position: the all-important, bullet-like tuck. Thighs parallel to the ground, chest mashed against thighs, hands stretched together out front, head cranked up just enough to see the track ahead and the tails of Jamie's skis as I gained on him. Ponytail streaming out the back of my thick wool hat, runny nose connected to frozen lip, chin frozen to jacket zipper, I must have looked like a possessed elf. I felt myself closing the gap then passing Jamie, and reveled in a split second of triumph as I saw his surprised expression.

By the time I returned my gaze forward, reality snatched the moment. One ski caught its edge and darted behind me, while the rest of my speeding body continued forward. Then came a brief, strangely peaceful moment midair where time stood still. I would revisit moments like this many times on many mountains but just this once, unaware of what inevitably followed, I marveled at its serenity. Then came the impact, an epic beater, a rag doll display of cartwheeling and bouncing down the trail. Skis and poles flew in every direction. I felt like I was in a giant washing machine, turning over and over. I finally came to rest right where the steeps melted into flats. Jamie, who had abruptly stood up and slowed to witness the spectacle, was now at my side.

"Are you all right?" he panted. Momentarily speechless and still appraising my health, he continued, "That was the best wipeout I've ever seen."

I glowed with pride. It was not the victory I'd planned, but it was every bit as satisfying. Franz Klammer just had his next disciple, and her name was Olivia Sharp.

Chapter 1:
The Big Time

A steep hillside in Switzerland, February 1987

The engine of the boxy blue van whined in protest, but our driver kept the accelerator pegged. When the narrow road flattened a bit he shifted up, accelerating over a crest and giving the engine a much needed break.

"Halfway up this bad boy!" Sean, our trainer smiled over at Anna and me, his eyes alive with the thrill of nearly flipping the rented cargo van at every corner. Within seconds he downshifted again, torturing the engine as we headed into another sharp left hand switchback. In the summer, grapevines covered this entire side of the valley, but in the dead of winter, the hillside was nothing but gray snow, smudged from the gravel and grit that spit from beneath every vehicle that huffed its way up the road.

Some of the girls on our team would have been feeling ill by now, but Anna used the opportunity to heave her weight to the passenger side and pin me against the door. I reached up and grabbed a handle that hung down from the roof. I used to play the same game in our station wagon as a kid. Then, I would get crushed by three heavier and unforgiving siblings. But now, with a solid 20 years of experience at creating breathing room, I could hold my own. I braced my feet against the floorboard and the door and pushed against Anna as hard as I could, sending her across the bench seat into Sean's shoulder and sending the van into a speed wobble.

Sean rolled his eyes without looking over. "Will you two ever grow up?"

"Look who's talking Mario Andretti!" Anna shot back. "You are responsible for precious cargo, not to mention us, and you're pretending this is a road rally." She reached to turn up the radio. The overly enthusiastic French-speaking disc jockey had relinquished the airwaves to The Bangles' *Walk Like an Egyptian* that now blared from the tinny speakers.

Sean tapped his fingers to the music on the steering wheel and didn't bother with a comeback. "Sometimes I love driving in Europe," he mused. And in all fairness, we chose to drive with him, crazy corners and all, rather than with the rest of the girls in the passenger van. In between scaring us to death, which we were well used to after three years of criss-crossing the European Alps with the US Ski Team, Sean always gave us some good laughs. At 25 he was the youngest of all our coaches, only five years older than Anna and me. And he was boyishly, innocently cute, which helped. Besides, what's a little near death experience between friends?

As we made our way up the steep hillside, the snowbanks got deeper, which was some comfort considering the precipitous drop on the other side of the ridiculously small guard rail. When my side of the van was on the outside, I could see down to the rooftops and church steeples of Swiss villages that dotted the Rhone Valley floor all the way west to Lake Geneva. Ahead of us the road flattened and widened again, letting us relax momentarily. The conversation turned to our destination and what we were about to experience.

Sean took one hand off the wheel long enough to turn down the radio and assumed an uncharacteristically sincere tone. "You know, if this was next year you'd be going to the Olympics." Of course we knew that. Everyone knew that. Even if we weren't talking about it, the Olympics were somewhere at the front or back of every coach and athlete's mind. This, the spectacle we were approaching in our trusty overloaded van, was the 1987 World Alpine Skiing Championships.

Over the next two weeks, the top men and women skiers in the world would break from the normal World Cup schedule to compete for World Champion titles in each of the five Alpine events: Downhill, Super G, Giant Slalom, Slalom and Combined. It would be sort of like a dress rehearsal for the Olympics, with the same competitors, the same events and the same level of competition. The only difference is that while the whole world tunes in to the Olympics, hardly anyone outside the ski world pays attention to the World Championships. Still, being here meant we were the best ski racers in the country, and it was an honor we were just starting to comprehend. None of us in the van, including Sean, had ever been at such an important event.

"This is a big deal," he added, as if we needed clarification. "You should be proud of yourselves."

Instinctively, I deflected the compliment. "I can't wait to see the hotel. I heard they always put you up in really good ones at the Champs."

"Donna will have taken the best room already. Guaranteed." Anna wasn't trying to burst my bubble. She was just stating the obvious. Donna was the team's assumed queen, who elevated "looking out for number 1" to an art form. Her father, a disturbingly tan real estate agent with an extraordinary amount of free time, practically went on tour with Donna, taking on the role of agent, coach, and sports psychologist for "Team Donna." He said things like, "We had a good race today," and "We need to focus on our slalom to get back on track," as if it was really him out there in the starting gate. He didn't know the first thing about ski technique, but he knew a lot about negotiation. Under his guidance Donna had become the master of getting exactly what she needed, no matter who she had to step on to get it.

"Yeah, she's probably already napping," I agreed, "...in a single."

A single room was a luxury when traveling with a team, a reward usually reserved for the top performers, and only then on rare occasions.

"At least she'll be with all her friends."

"Easy, killers," Sean interrupted. "Dan already made out the rooming list. And it's not like we're going to suffer. Dan says this place rocks. He coached here back in the day." The day, being the time just before my generation of skiers, when Dan led a fierce US Ski Team that won five medals at the 1984 Sarajevo Olympics. That team became the gold standard to which our young team was always compared. So far, we came up shamefully short.

Sean continued: "But we're not going to the hotel just yet. First we have to go to the race office and get accredited. You know, sign an oath, pee in a cup, gender testing…"

"What?!" we yelled in unison, causing Sean to flinch. Peeing in a cup for drug testing we understood. But gender testing?

"I'm *not* pulling my pants down in front of some gnarly old Swiss guy!" The vision Anna conjured up made me squirm and reflexively check my zipper.

When Sean stopped laughing he explained, "Don't worry. I think they just have to scrape a cheek cell or something, and check it for the female chromosome."

"And why do they have to do that?" Anna demanded.

"Apparently a few years back there was an Erika who won some medals but turned out to be an Erik, so now they check the women at every major event. You know those Euros and their ski racing. They'll do anything to win."

We did know those Euros pretty well by now. Ski racing is like a religion to them, like football in the States. And, like NFL stars, the Swiss and Austrian skiers appeared on billboards and cereal boxes, in magazines and store displays, hawking everything from office products and banks to sports drinks and candy bars. Their lives were the topics of newspaper headlines and TV talk shows. Just attending the World Championships in Switzerland, on a year when the Swiss were dominating the World Cup circuit, was going to be like going to Disney World on spring break. I hadn't let myself imagine what it would feel like to compete on that stage. Until now.

Sean reached for the radio again, perhaps hoping to get all our minds off the topics of gender testing and bloodthirsty competition.

"Perfect!" he smiled, cranking the volume as high as it would go. The opening strains of *The Final Countdown*, the cheesy anthem of the moment, ironically by a band called Europe, trumpeted through the speakers. We all joined in, swaying heads and shoulders to the beat, drumming the dashboard and belting out the chorus as loud as we could.

For the last kilometer we had been stuck behind an overloaded Fiat Panda, which crawled along slower than our hog of a cargo van. As soon as we were on the sunny plateau and hit a straightaway, Sean downshifted once more and pulled out next to the Fiat, winding out the engine as we squeezed past a road sign with one black car and one red car next to it, the universal sign for "No Passing Zone." We tucked back into our lane just in front of a bakery truck that was coming right at us in the opposite direction.

The road made one final curve before delivering us smack into a burst of civilization. Sean slammed on the brakes. Suddenly the road was clogged, not only with cars but also with fur coats ambling in and out of fancy watch shops, cafes and chocolatier boutiques. We drove directly under a huge "Wilkommen/Beinvenue" banner stretched across the road. "1987 Ski Alpine Welt Meister / 1987 Championnats du Ski Alpin" it advertised. Sean saw a "Rennburo" sign with an arrow and swerved into a tiny sidestreet in search of the race headquarters. After a few more turns he parked the van in front of a school plastered with World Championship banners and mobbed with athletes, coaches and officials.

"Girls. Welcome to the big time!"

Chapter 2:
Swiss Cheeses

An hour later, Anna and I had finally hauled ourselves and our huge duffel bags up to our third floor room. Large photo credentials hung around our necks, and we each had a gift bag full of various trinkets, Swiss cowbells, chocolate, t-shirts, hats and two scrolls of paper. I left the official certificate of participation rolled up, but unfurled the other one and held it up in triumph.

"I am officially female. Finally, we can get in to Ladies Night anywhere!"

"Don't laugh," Anna said. "That's the kind of thing my mom would frame." Anna's mom still thought we should have a dress code for travel, and hated that her beautiful, perfectly-groomed daughter, who looked so nice in her tennis whites at "The Club" in one of Denver's toniest suburbs, now spent most of her life in sweats and t-shirts. To be sure, Anna's life would be very different right now if she'd accepted any of the tennis scholarships she'd been offered at nice, sunny colleges like U. C. San Diego. We all had our choices along the way. But somehow traveling to remote mountain villages in grubby vans to pursue a physically punishing and dangerous sport nobody in our country knew or cared a thing about had won. Go figure.

It didn't take us long to unpack in our spacious, luxurious room. At World Cup races, the host area paid for our lodging, but at the World Championships each national federation had to pay for its own lodging. The US Ski Team pulled out all the stops for big events, largely because the Trustees were on hand. The Trustees were composed mostly of wealthy, savvy businessmen who had a weakness for elite sports, a weakness they indulged by spending lots of money on the US Ski Team. In return they got an official team uniform and a back stage pass with us at these major events. It seemed like a fair enough trade, especially at times like this when only the finest hotel would do.

I didn't really care what the room was like as long as it was warm and the beds were comfortable. This sunny, south-facing room had a huge bathroom with heated floors and a porch with a panoramic view of the Valais Alps on the other side of the Rhone Valley. Inside the large armoire was a big TV and plenty of space to hang the sleek, long, powder blue coats our clothing sponsor gave us to wear in the opening parade.

I liked rooming with Anna because it didn't take any extra energy. First of all, we were both "speed skiers," which meant we skied chiefly Downhill and Super G, the speed events. "Tech skiers" specialized in slalom and giant slalom, the lower speed, turnier technical events. "Speed" and "tech" skiers not only had different schedules but, on our team at least, they tended to have different personalities as well. The tech skiers were more high-strung and particular about everything from breakfast to music selection. Speed skiers tended to be a little looser all the way around, and Anna especially had always served as a much-needed pressure release valve, finding humor in even the worst situations. We never had to tiptoe around each other or worry about invading each other's space. And even though Anna had a serious boyfriend she had the decency not to set up a photo shrine next to the bed.

Best of all, Anna never hogged the phone. Calling home from Europe was expensive enough even if you did it from a phone booth in the local post office. It cost more from the hotel lobby and was downright outrageous from your hotel room. Just the past summer, one rookie coach racked up a $400 bill in three calls home to his wife. But incoming calls were another matter, and rooming with someone who fielded nightly, brooding calls from distant boyfriends was torture. Romantically, Anna lived in the moment, which meant not giving out her phone numbers in Europe. Most of our communication home was via postcards. We only called home if we got hurt or did really well in a race. So far on this trip neither had happened. Our families followed our race results by calling the US Ski Team hotline, which had a recorded message with all the results for men and women, World Cup and Europa Cup races.

We did both call home when we learned we'd made the World Championship team. My family couldn't scramble to make the trip over and Anna's never considered it, which was sort of a bummer. But not having to coordinate afternoon and evening visits with an entourage of friends and family certainly simplified things. Once we lay down on our beds, however, I did think of someone I wanted to call.

"We should call Nellie and tell her we're officially girls. She'd like that."

Nellie had come up the ranks of the US Ski Team with Anna and me. Even though she was a technical skier, a one-time sensation bred for optimal performance at an intense Vermont ski academy, we had discovered early on that she was "one of us," low maintenance in the scheme of things. Nellie and I had recovered from our first knee injuries together three years earlier. Reinjuring our knees the following year cemented our bond.

But last fall, in what seemed like a freak accident, she had blown out the ligaments in her knee yet again. This time, her first call from the hospital was to the ski coach at CU, the University of Colorado in Boulder. He let her enroll on a scholarship that winter so that she could ski for their team the following year. That bought her some time to recover and to try to get back on the team the following summer, before the Olympics. I still couldn't believe that seven years after first hearing about Nellie Lukovic, the "great young hope" for US skiing, I was at the World Championships alongside the world's best skiers, and she was fighting just for a spot on the national team.

"I don't even know her number now," Anna said. "Remember she moved into the dorms after Christmas break?"

"That's right. Well, let's write her a postcard and send it to the CU team office. They'll get it to her."

The World Championships are a long, drawn out event with a separate day for each of the five events, for men and women. Also, they scheduled in extra training days for the downhill, the premiere spectator and TV event, both to insure against weather delays and to allow each team to pick their fastest racers. Every downhill race is preceded by at least two days of training on the course, so that athletes can familiarize themselves with the hill before plunging down it full speed, at anywhere from 60-80 plus miles per hour. At Olympic and World Championship events, each country can run up to six athletes in downhill training and use those times to determine a "final four" who get to race. Before we could take on the rest of the world Anna and I first had to battle each other and our teammates for a starting spot. The plush hotel room and fanfare did come with a price tag, and that was added stress.

So far, competition pressure hadn't ever gotten in the way of Anna and me having a good time, not as 13-year-olds in our first Jr. Olympics together and not now. We were eager to get into the busy, noisy streets, to immerse ourselves in the scene. As I pulled open the heavy glass front door of our hotel, a voice called to us:

"Meeting at 6:15. Dinner at 7!" Ken. We knew his voice and didn't bother to turn around. Anna put up her hand in a sort of wave that also could have meant, "whatever." We didn't really care how the head coach of the entire team interpreted the gesture. Every step of our way, he had been there, trying to trip us up when nobody was looking, then reluctantly offering us a hand when nobody better showed up to take our places. We'd made it here despite his best efforts. We continued out the door and took a deep breath of fresh air before heading towards the excitement, the action, the fun—in other words, a Ken-free zone.

Our hotel was tucked away from the main street but only moments from the center of town. Getting down the sidewalk in town meant dodging couples in his and her fur coats and tall apres ski boots, who stopped to inspect the watch and jewelry displays in the store windows, and immaculately dressed European families strolling in and out of cafes and sports shops. All the World Cups were in well-known resorts, but it took a really fancy resort with lots of money to spend to secure a World Championships bid. Every once in a while the entire street was overtaken by a boisterous crowd—people clanging large cowbells, singing and waving homemade signs with blown-up pictures of a favorite Swiss ski star. The various fan clubs—with their painted faces, costumes and air horns— showed up in some form at every World Cup, but here they appeared en masse, advancing through the narrow streets like small armies, behind banners made of decorated bedsheets, stopping all traffic as they oozed past.

This year the Swiss fans had many stars to choose from, on both the men's and women's teams and in every event. And they even could pick sides in the media-hyped rivalry between their two top female speed skiers: the composed, polite veteran Maria Walliser from the German speaking part of Switzerland who answered every question with eloquence and a smile; or fiery Michaela Figini from the Italian-speaking region—a phenom who won the downhill gold in 1984 at only 17 years of age— who didn't seem to care what the press thought of her. The two had taken turns winning nearly every speed race so far that season. Whether or not they really disliked each other barely mattered as far as the press was concerned. Harmony is boring, conflict sells. Nearly every day a headline or picture of them graced the cover of the *Blick*, Switzerland's daily version of the *National Enquirer*.

Anna and I were both staring at a guy dressed in what looked like a wooly yak suit, complete with matted fur, horns and huge, scary bug-eyes. He looked alarmingly similar to the notorious Yugoslavian fans that tended to swig too much Slivovich (the local firewater) to prep for race days when the World Cup visited their home country in Maribor. It was not unusual to be pelted with empty beer bottles by such characters as we rode the Poma lift. Anna's expression switched instantly from concern to delight when she saw a familiar face.

"Hey, there's Goose!" Just beyond yak guy—flattened against the wall to get out of yak guy's way in fact—stood our old coach. Old as in former, not as in old. Gus (it sounded like goose in German, so that's the way we said it) was only in his late Twenties, but he was my first real US Ski Team coach and by far the best one I'd ever had. He had been Ken's assistant two years earlier during my rookie year on the Europa Cup circuit—the farm league for the World Cup. It hadn't taken long to figure out who really should have been in charge.

Ken's only real claim to fame was that he had coached Donna at the academy the year she made the US Ski Team. According to Ken, he not only coached her but "made her who she was," a preposterous concept considering how little "making" there was left to do with Donna in the brief intersection of their time together. Nonetheless, he never hesitated to make the association with his appearance and her success. As long as he made her life easy by leaving her alone, she never bothered to refute his claims. So the rest of us were stuck with Ken, who dispensed his coaching advice robotically, like some sort of button-activated action figure—"Don't sit back. Don't rotate. Don't lean in." Meanwhile, Gus guided us like Yoda, telling us what *to* do instead of what *not* to do. He bestowed his quiet wisdom in simple terms, with a few missing words and German prepositions: "Soften the ankles and roll over them mit the k-nees. Move over the terrain, mit feeling. Go for, you can do!"

With his un-English sentence structure ("Can you me the coffee pass?") and sing-songy Swiss accent, Gus even sounded like Yoda. Whatever he lacked in language skills he more than made up for in technical knowledge and real athletic experience. That first exposure to the cutthroat competition on the Europa Cup is critical for a young ski racer, and Gus was like our Guardian Angel, making sure we held our heads high and learned from our potentially crushing losses.

As long as Gus was around to make things work smoothly on and off the hill, Ken seemed like a harmless, bumbling, cartoon character. But after one season, when it became obvious Gus couldn't work under Ken, the US Ski Team's director of the moment (who Ken spent most of his time sucking up to), fired Gus and promoted Ken to head coach. Within days Gus was snapped up to lead the Swiss technical team. Every time I saw him in the shiny silver and red Swiss uniform it stung a little, because he was our good thing first.

When Gus spotted us his serious expression softened, and a wide smile spread across his face as he came towards us. He gave us each a big hug and I got a whiff of his familiar gaminess, a mixture of sweat and coffee, hundreds of smoky ski lodges, and maybe a fondue stube or two. Deodorant and laundry were never his strong points, but somehow that never mattered. He always made me feel good.

"Servus! Wie Geht's—how you doo-ink?" Gus asked.

"You two at the champs." He nodded his head and looked impressed. "Congratulieren. I knew you could do!"

Gus looked good, but tired. Coaching for the Swiss team during these World Championships, when the country expected multiple medals in every event as a warm up to the Olympics, had to be one of the most stressful jobs in sport. We chatted a bit about Nellie's latest injury and the other girls, and he told us some things about the race hill. When we mentioned that Ken was back at the hotel babysitting the Trustees, he only rolled his eyes and made a face like he was remembering an especially bad meal.

"Well girls, I go now to the coaches' meeting. I'm the big cheese you know." He winked at our shared joke. He remembered how Ken had once referred to himself as the Big Cheese, so we nicknamed him *The Cheeseball* and the name had stuck.

"Remember girls. Dis here…" and he waved his arm in a circle to include the banners, the awards plaza, and the crowded streets, "Dis is for the experience girls. Only the experience. Don't to get caught up in dis. Patience for you. Patience!"

After Gus left we started to walk into a café, but Anna put her arm out and stopped my hand from opening the door. I followed her eyes and understood immediately. Lucy, our big-haired teammate was easy to spot and easier to hear as she held court with some friends from home who had come to watch her in the downhill event. Based on a surprise win earlier in the season, Lucy had one of the two secure race spots in the downhill. And based on that same win her head had increased in size significantly, which was saying a lot. The last thing either of us wanted was to hear more about Lucy from Lucy, so we backed away from the door and doubled back the way we'd come.

An hour later Lucy and the rest of our teammates—10 of us in all—gathered in the hotel lobby and settled into plush sofas and overstuffed chairs. We were joined by the coaches and all the equipment representatives (reps) who travel with the World Cup Team to prepare and maintain the gear their companies provide. Each ski, boot, binding and even goggle company provided at least one rep. That brought the women's team entourage to about 25 people, not counting all the friends, families and Trustees who were there for support.

Ken was in his "dress" jeans and the cowboy boots that made him an inch taller. After handing out some more loot—new turtlenecks and long johns from one of our sponsors—he ran down the schedule for the next day, including the Opening Ceremonies the following evening. After going over all the details he put down the paper he'd been reading from and cleared his throat. This, we all recognized with dread, was Ken switching gears. Ever so softly, someone groaned.

"Goody! Here comes the speech," Anna whispered beside me, digging her elbow into my side. Ken loved big dramatic speeches and a big event like this was a perfect opportunity to give one.

"Each of you is here because you are one of the best skiers in the country. You not only represent the US Ski Team but also the entire country. As a top athlete, you are expected to conduct yourselves appropriately. I know a lot of you have friends and family here, and that the men's team is here as well. Those are all distractions...." He went into detail then, ticking off all the fun things we were supposed to avoid and even suggested a curfew on race nights.

Anna whispered again: "Do you think he's going to tuck us in at night?" Before I could answer, Ken was already off bedtime rules and on to his favorite topic—medals.

"The Olympics are one year away. This is your chance to show the world we're ready. This is where we show what we're made of, that we're tougher than everyone else, that we work harder than everyone else. We won five medals at the last Olympics, and four medals at the last World Championships. We can do the same here, or better...."

I couldn't help thinking back to what Gus had said. "Patience." I had, after all, been on the World Cup circuit for exactly one month. Anna had been on it almost one whole season. Our team had one thin top tier of "A-Team" vets—none of whom needed to be told how to win a medal; a smattering of "B-Team" up and comers who had some international racing success but were long shots at medals; and a whole lot of "C-Team" rookies, like me, who needed experience more than speeches.

As I looked around the room, it was clear nobody was paying Ken the slightest bit of attention. Natalie, the most successful US skier ever and possibly the most respected female skier on the entire circuit, glanced down at her watch occasionally. Linda, who already owned one gold medal, looked on politely but couldn't help stifling a yawn. Donna, who at 16 years of age had become the youngest ever World Cup winner, didn't listen to anyone but herself, and by the way she was intently twirling her hair around her index finger it was clear she wasn't making an exception tonight. Lucy—the great downhill hope—kept shooting apologetic looks to her friends who were already seated in the dining room. The rest of us had heard enough of Ken's speeches on our way up the ranks alongside him, and instinctively tuned out.

It appeared that Ken was giving this speech entirely for his own benefit, until I looked behind me at the bar. There several of the Trustees had gathered in their still-creased new turtlenecks to listen earnestly. They looked serious, and nodded approvingly every time Ken brought up medals and winning and champions. That's what they wanted to hear. That's why they paid the money.

After the meeting broke up, Anna and I headed through the bar area and into the dining room. Our table had a good view back through the lobby, where Donna lingered, all dressed up and clearly ready for action. Her perfectly blow-dried blond mane glistened and rested lightly on her white coat. Lit from behind as she was from the floor lamp, she almost appeared to have a halo. That look and that presence made me understand why people had started calling her Ma-donna, and it reminded me why she made me alternately insanely jealous and mildly nauseous. Moments later, a young, handsome, rising star on the Italian team arrived. Donna got up immediately, shook her hair in one smooth arc, hooked her arm in his and walked out the door. From the far side of the bar, her father registered the departure with a satisfied smile and returned his attention to a glass of chilled white wine.

The rest of us settled for dinner "in" which was a far cry from our ordinary road fare. Here we dined rather than ate. Four courses arrived on trays borne by polite waiters in crisp white shirts. It took forever, because of the elaborate service and because we were enjoying the company of two boys, one of them the black-haired, blue-eyed Blake, my perpetual crush. Anna had the kind of assuredness that comes with having a serious boyfriend at home, the kind of assuredness that made her attractive to boys like Blake. His roommate Eric, who was built like a Mack truck and skied like one too, always made me laugh, which eased the pain I might have otherwise felt at Blake's obvious interest in Anna. Blake and Eric were also downhillers, but Blake had already secured his race spot, so he was a little more relaxed than usual. Eric, a totally unproven rookie, was on the hot spot like Anna and me, but he simply loved speed and didn't know the meaning of the word stress. They were perfect dinner partners.

The Trustees hung out in the hotel bar, sipping golden beers from tall glasses and quizzing the coaches about our medal chances. Most of the coaches skirted the question as best they could, but Ken fed the fire with his "medal speak" as often as he could. His job as cheeseball-in-chief depended on it. After dinner Anna, Blake, Eric and I made our way past the bar. The most intense Type-A-from-Hell trustee, Phil, stood at the end. The stock market tycoon and terminally frustrated athlete loved to opine on elite sports, and was deep in conversation with another trustee. I tried to slip past him, but he flagged me down: "Hey Sharpie!"

Damn! I was snared. Phil "owned" me in a way. That year the ski team, in a bid to wring more money from the people who already paid them ridiculous sums of it, came up with a brilliant plan. For an extra $10,000 you could "buy" an athlete for the year, sort of like sponsoring an orphan in a third world country. In return that athlete would send you postcards and letters... and apparently hang out with you at big events. Phil had bought me, but since it was a lottery style assignment, I knew he felt like he'd been ripped off. At the very least, I had to talk to him when asked, so I turned to him and smiled like we were old friends

"Hi Phil! How was your trip?" He smiled and put his arm around me in a fatherly way, like he was proud. At least I had made the World Championships for God's sake, so his investment wasn't a complete loss.

"You have the inside scoop. Who's hot? Who's the new one to watch?" Phil said it as if it certainly wasn't me.

"Well, Lucy has been skiing really well. And Donna."

He grinned and rolled his eyes knowingly at the other trustee.

"They've been around. I mean who's up and coming. Who's our next Erica Hess or Michaela Figini?" The fact that he brought up those two Swiss stars in particular revealed Phil's cluelessness. Even in Switzerland, where ski champions practically grow by the mound like potatoes, the teenage success of those skiers was deemed as nothing short of miraculous. But guys like Phil who craved instant success eagerly latched on to miracles as case studies. I was tempted to give him the same speech Gus had given me two years earlier after my second knee injury—the speech that included, in his signature blend of English and German, the following perfectly clear points: that young superstars, who win World Cups and medals in their teens, are a rare gift; that you can't build a team around stars that may burn bright or burn out; that you need grunts like Anna, Lucy and me who move up the ranks at a boring steady pace to create depth and stability on a team; that as an individual and as a team you need patience to build strength. But I knew he'd never get it. I couldn't help feeling that he wanted to trade us all in for younger, flashier models. Before I could come up with an answer, he continued:"Where's Greta anyway?"

"Oh, Greta?" I couldn't resist adding, "You mean Greta the Great?"

At 16 years of age Greta had been anointed as the US Ski Team's next big star. With her perfect dimples and a gymnast's body that seemed genetically engineered for athletic excellence, she was the poster child for the future of the sport in our country, just as Nellie had once been. In fact her smiling face was already on posters and in ads for various US Ski Team sponsors and even on the sides of city buses in Utah advertising the "Greatest Snow on Earth." Two years later, she had yet to make her mark in any international competition because she crumbled whenever she got to the Europa Cup and came face-to-face with the down and dirty, dog-eat-dog competition in Europe. She might be great some day but she needed time, like everyone else.

"I don't know where Greta is," I told Phil, "but she's not here." As I walked away I added quietly, "We're the best you've got."

Chapter 3:
My Place In The Sun

Even though early February was still technically the dead of winter, the Alps were having a spell of warm, clear weather. From the mountaintop start of the downhill course, the Swiss Alps spread out like a scene from a cereal box. Jagged white peaks stretched in all directions, cutting like serrated teeth into an impossibly blue sky. In front of this backdrop, all the teams gathered in small clutches of matching uniforms. One of the Swiss coaches stopped next to our powder blue-clad tribe and pointed to where the Matterhorn and Mont Blanc poked up on the horizon. On postcard perfect mornings like this, everybody with a pulse would want to be a downhiller. We were all in good cheer when we set out for our first look at the course, or "inspection" as it is officially called.

Inspection is when you look at the course before running it and pick your line (your ideal path through the gates). It's also your only chance to examine the various terrain features like bumps and sidehills and icy patches before you're zinging across them *mach schnell*, really fast in any language. On any subsequent inspections—we usually got one per day until the race—each racer would go down the course on her own, stopping at each coach in his position along the course to talk about how to best ski just that particular section. But we always took the first inspection together as a team.

The only good thing about Ken being the head coach was that it seriously limited his time on the hill. Once the official training and competition began, Ken spent most of his time snarled in logistical arrangements concerning the Trustees, sponsors and press obligations. He left the coaching to our "real" coaches—Sepp, the head speed team coach, and Dan, the head technical team coach. Both had joined the team the previous spring. I had only graduated to the World Cup team in January, so I was still getting to know them. Sepp, who had started his coaching career at a US academy then moved around the world as a private coach, came to us most recently from the Austrian women's team. Though we never knew why he was suddenly available for hire he clearly worked best in an unstructured environment. Dan was on his second stint as a US Ski Team coach. After the last Olympics he had left the national team and scored a prime, high paying, stay-at-home position as headmaster at a top ski academy. He didn't exactly want to come back to the US Ski Team, especially since he'd left as a hero after '84. But after Gus left and Ken slithered into his position of power, some of the team veterans had nearly begged Dan to return. Unlike the Cheeseball, who had pursued his position for his ego, Dan took his job out of a sense of duty.

Eight of us—six dowhillers plus our top two technical skiers, Donna and Natalie, who would be skiing a slightly shortened version of the downhill course as part of the Combined (part downhill, part slalom) event—followed

Sepp, Dan and two other assistant coaches through the start shack. We formed a loose line as we slid our skis past some gates that led us gently back and forth down the long, flat top section. Up ahead, the course turned sharply left, then disappeared. All that was visible from where we stood was the top edge of a massive section of orange safety netting, a sure sign of what was below. Anna scooted ahead to the last red gate and looked over the edge.

"Yup." She pointed her pole downhill. "Behold the tuna turn!" Pretty much every downhill had at least one tuna turn, so called because if you came into it too fast and couldn't hold your line you ended up caught in the net, like a giant tuna.

We all slid down to her position and looked downhill to see one row of 20-foot high orange fencing that lined the edge of the slope alongside a huge left turn, to the top of a sharp knoll. Beyond that, we saw just the top of another set of fencing.

"It's a double!" Anna continued. I was glad I had goggles on, because maybe nobody would see how nervous I was. If there were already two tuna turns in the first thirty seconds, it promised to be a pretty hairy course, not that I was a great judge of World Cup courses. So far I'd raced in all of three. I wondered if anyone else was nervous. As if in answer, Lucy let out a sort of war cry and pushed over the edge, accelerating down the hill, a thick ponytail of black curls streaming in the wind from the back of her helmet. At the top of the next drop-off she slid her skis sideways, coming to a hockey stop in a cloud of snow spray.

We followed one by one, then made our way down the rest of the course slowly, studying every gate and every angle of terrain, discussing where to start each turn and how to take each jump (or "chump" as Sepp pronounced them) to minimize the launch. A familiar sense of dread took hold and widened like a black hole in my stomach. This, I was beginning to understand, was my "normal" reaction to seeing a tough downhill for the first time. Maybe someday I'd be like Lucy, eager to get in the starting gate and throw myself down a new course. But for now I understood my body, still fresh from repairing itself, took a lot more convincing. I knew that once I got through the starting gate, the fear would be replaced by a rush of adrenaline, and after crossing the finish I'd want to get right back up the hill and do it again. But the space between now and then was torturous.

At the end of our inspection run, we each found a quiet spot in the flat finish arena to mentally rehearse the entire course while it was still fresh in our minds. I opened my eyes, looked back up the final steep pitch that led into the finish stadium and asked whatever higher power might be listening, "Just let me get through the first run."

Fortunately it was a warm day, and the sun still shone brightly on the track when I took my run which was, in my mind, perfect—not particularly fast, but without incident. The course was tough but good, and even fun once you got through the tuna turns and the two big jumps that followed. In a little less than two minutes it plunged you from the treeless summit all the way down to the village 2,500 vertical feet below. At the bottom I was out of breath but exhilarated and, more than anything else, relieved.

That night after dinner, I sat down to my first interview

with Howard Nicks, the towering, white-haired ski writer who often traveled with the team. Howard had been around longer than any racer or coach could remember, possibly since the last Ice Age, and with his exhaustive interviewing skills had built an encyclopedic knowledge of every World Cup competitor from every team. His favorite subjects were underdogs, and he was thrilled that we were staying in the same hotel as the Russian and Czechoslovakian teams. Both countries were fielding a small team of athletes, most of them rookies, in the hopes of creating some medal contenders by next year's Olympics. It was a late but sincere effort.

I was so new to the World Cup circuit that Howard had no scoop on me. He was never without his two compact media guidebooks—one for the World Cup athletes and one for the US Ski Team athletes. They were sort of a cheat sheet for journalists, with head shots, vital stats and background tidbits on all the athletes of potential interest. I didn't show up in either book. Now that I was here, he had to do his homework quickly just in case I a:) qualified to race b:) "came from nowhere" to win a medal, or c:) crashed horrifically. All of the above were newsworthy. We settled into a quiet corner with plates of flaky apple strudel "mit schlag," topped with whipped cream. The first thing Howard asked me had nothing to do with ski racing:

"I hear you graduated from high school at 15. Why were you in such a rush?" Most reporters started with standard career info like hometown, ski club and how many years you'd been on the team. Howard was old school. His profiles were real stories. So, instead of asking about my goals and whether or not I planned on winning a medal—the things every athlete here had in common—

he asked questions that might reveal what made Olivia Sharp different.

I explained my father's love for skiing and my mother's love for anything my father loved and how, from the time I was born, we had piled into the station wagon and driven eight hours every winter weekend to go from suburban California to the Sierra Nevada Mountains and back. When he found out my great, great grandmother had crossed those same mountains to get to California before the Gold Rush, he got excited and jotted notes while exclaiming: "Real covered wagon stock!"

I described how, as the youngest of four, I was always trying to keep up, thus my downhill racing skills were born of necessity. So too were my accelerated academics. I had started kindergarten a year young; then, when we finally moved from the flatlands to the mountains I skipped a grade to be in the same school as my siblings. Howard stopped me.

"Wasn't that a bit awkward, you know, socially?" I took a moment to consider how I could even begin to describe how right he was on that.

"Have you ever seen how well a 12-year-old fits into a high school garbage can?" I finally replied. He nodded, and cringed.

I joked about starting high school as a shy and woefully underdeveloped 12-year-old, but it was entering middle school in a new community at nine years of age that was truly hellish. I'm not sure what was worse: the towering eighth grade boys who dumped my locker contents onto the floor every day for fun, getting picked last for every team activity or having to change for gym next to the bodacious D-cup Roxanne Nielsen. Fortunately, nothing that happened in school caused any lasting damage because I had one sanctuary where I always fit in. That place was on the ski mountain, at Squaw Valley USA.

There is not likely any Squaw Valley outside of the USA but Alex Cushing, the ski area's owner and founder thought "USA" brought an appropriate level of respect to a place that had once hosted the Olympics. Howard had actually reported on the Squaw Valley Olympics in 1960, before I was born, and knew many of the French, Swiss, Austrian, Scandinavian and Argentine athletes who stayed on in Squaw after the Games. Many of them ended up coaching me, and the long list of World Class skiers that Squaw produced. We talked about what a gift it was to grow up surrounded by such a collection of magically gifted athletes who, despite wildly different backgrounds and accents, all spoke the same language of skiing.

In answer to his first question, I had graduated from high school at 15, in January of my senior year, because I wanted to concentrate on making the US Ski Team. It was a circuitous path. What I had anticipated as a young phenom—an express route to glory—had somewhere along the way turned into something more like Mr. Toad's Wild Ride. The bumpy trail of false summits, potholes and dead ends had me chasing races across the country, cramming into station wagons with near strangers, spending sub zero nights in unheated cabins and foraging for abandoned lunches in coin lockers. This, of course, after I had turned down generous offers from college recruiters.

Finally, after two years and what felt like an eternity of shouting "Pick me! Pick me!", the US Ski Team coaches assured me I was next in line for the downhill team. And that's when the injuries started. I told Howard what it was like to watch the last Olympics from a hospital bed, high on morphine after knee surgery, and how it felt even more hopeless to be back in that hospital bed again a year later.

"It takes a lot of nerve to go right back to downhill racing after all those injuries," Howard suggested.

"I didn't. Ken decided I was 'too smart' to be a downhiller. "

"What does that mean?" Howard asked.

"I don't know what *he* meant by it, but to me it meant I had to learn how to ski slalom really fast if I wanted to get back on the team."

"Ahh, a renaissance skier." Howard scratched away on his notepad.

"Not really. I'm not exactly a fast-twitch kind of girl, but I faked it pretty well." I explained how last summer Dan and Sepp had decided to get me back to downhill racing, slowly easing me back to speed at my own pace. Returning to the speed team had felt like taking off a tight, fitted blazer and putting on a favorite sweatshirt. Finally, at 20 years old, I was healthy and with coaches who believed in me. Immediately things started to click.

"So really, with all that time off, in ski racing years you're more like a 17-year-old," Howard offered. I liked his perspective. I wasn't inexperienced. I was just unusually fresh for my age.

I had always loved reading Howard's stories because he didn't just tell the facts—he told a story. He crafted those stories through his genuine understanding that everybody comes from "somewhere," and that the buried details are often the most revealing part of the story. After an interview with Howard you felt like you knew yourself better.

Towards the end of our meeting, we finally talked about the race.

"Are you excited to race in your first World Championships?" I loved Howard's optimism. Realistically, my chances seemed slim, especially after having seen how much faster Lucy's and Anna's training times were than mine.

"If I make it. There's Lucy and Anna for sure. And Linda is an automatic of course, so that leaves one spot for three of us. So *maybe*, if all goes well…" I trailed off.

"Have you ever heard the saying, 'It ain't over till the fat lady sings?' Don't count yourself out. Much stranger things have happened. Remember, you pioneers are tough." Howard looked at me in all seriousness to make sure I got it while I furrowed my brow and scooped the last bit of cinnamon-flecked whipped cream and strudel onto my fork.

"Howard, are you calling me fat?"

Howard was saved from answering by the arrival of Golnur Postnikova the big, blond Russian who smiled sweetly and skied as if being chased by wolves. She had taken a seat at the table next to us, and Howard couldn't resist the opportunity to chat with his favorite Eastern Block underdog. If I felt old at 20, Postnikova, at 22 years of age, was ancient by Russian standards. But even the Russian coaches knew how long it took to become a great downhiller, and she was the one they were grooming for Calgary. The rumor was that their government funded sports federation had built an exact replica of Calgary's Olympic downhill course somewhere in the Caucasus Mountains where she trained. So far she was on track, making rapid progress up the world rankings.

We stood up, and Howard shook my hand firmly.

"Miss Sharp. Good luck. I have a feeling we'll be having a lot more of these chats."

At the end of our second training day, high clouds crept like a thin layer of cotton across the bluebird sky. Lenticular clouds are a sure sign of incoming nasty weather. The next day we were only able to get one run on the course from the lower combined event start. The speeds were slightly lower, but it was much more difficult to run a course in flat light, where you could barely distinguish the gray line between air and snow. "Skiing inside a milk carton" is how we described runs like that, where it was nearly impossible to see the terrain changes and judge your speed. The only thing worse was when the fog rolled in, and we blindly felt our way down with our feet, ankles and knees. That was "skiing by Braille."

With the weather expected to worsen, the race organizers scheduled a final training day with two runs from the upper start so that whenever the skies cleared they would be ready to run either the Combined or Downhill event. On the first run, I was picked to be in the snow seed. The snow seed is a group of five racers picked at random from the end of the starting order. They run the course after the forerunners but before the first racers as extra insurance that the course is safe and fair. It's sort of like being a guinea pig. When there is any new snow on the course to slow your skis down, running in the snow seed is a huge disadvantage. Nevertheless, I always liked getting my run over and not having to hang around at the start. Also, I got to see more of the course from below and whatever I couldn't see I could watch on the Jumbotron with the rest of the spectators.

I watched the entire first seed of 15 racers. Three of the Swiss landed in the top five. Our first racer would be

Lucy, running 17th. I could barely make Lucy out as she rounded the last corner and came into view. She was crouched so low in her tuck that all I could clearly see were the two trails of snow, coming from behind her skis like smoke. I hated running downhill in flat light, but Lucy had no problem hurtling headlong down a mountain blindly. It helped that she had a screw loose (one of several unflattering reasons for her nickname, "Loose"), and that she had never had a problem with self-confidence. She certainly *looked* fast. When she crossed the finish line, her time flashed up on the scoreboard with an "01" next to it. Immediately the reporters swarmed around her, sticking microphones in her face or listening intently while scribbling in their small notebooks. She chatted excitedly while I watched the rest of my teammates take their runs. None fared well.

Earning a race spot would depend entirely on this next run, and I'd have to beat two girls—one of them Anna—for it. All season Anna had been solidly ahead of me, but now we were basically dead even. Both of us had one mulligan—a throwaway run—one decent run and one pretty sketchy inside-the-milk-carton run. Off the hill we still got along fine, but a force field of tension had crept between us. We spent less time in the room together and usually ate dinner with other people. As I headed to the chairlift for this deciding run, Anna deliberately scooted ahead of me and slid onto a chair.

Before I could follow on my own, Lucy flagged me down. Ugh. I wanted a moment of peace, alone on the chair, to collect myself. I was in no mood for chatter. But Lucy was the self-appointed mentor to every rookie on the speed team. She took it as her responsibility to impart her wisdom, louder and from closer range than necessary.

Getting in my face, literally, was her way of psyching me up.

"You can do it Sharpie!" She leaned in close to me, still giddy and amped from her run, but surprisingly sincere. I decided to listen, even patiently. She had, after all, just skied the course I needed to ace, as well as it could be skied.

"Just ski smart on the top through the tuna turns, then no matter what happens up there, let it fly on the bottom." She went on to describe her run in detail. Normally I tuned her out as too much information, but today I greedily absorbed every word. Lucy wasn't taking her final training run. Part of the psych game in downhill is not showing all your tricks. Often when racers know they are having a fast training run, they stand up and smear away speed before crossing the finish line, leaving the impression that they can go much faster on race day. And if they've run the course enough to have it wired, they sometimes skip the final training run. Lucy was in the big leagues now, and she was playing the game.

When I loaded the chair, blissfully alone, the drizzle had turned into fat wet snowflakes. By the time I reached the top of the course it had turned into "graupel," frozen pellets that look like fertilizer bits and feel like bullets when they pelt you. As if the conditions weren't nasty enough, the fog rolled in.

We waited in the mountaintop lodge while the coaches and course jury looked at the course to decide if it was safe. Hurry up and wait is among the first skills a downhiller masters. After half an hour, the coaches radioed to Sean that the run would resume, but at 30-second intervals. Running the racers so close was more dangerous—if anyone fell in the race line there was little chance to "yellow flag" the next racer off the course to stop her from piling in to the fallen racer. But the short interval would keep the track from filling up with snow and slowing down between racers, so it was also fairer to all competitors. And it would get this run over with, which was what everyone wanted.

I had the worst international downhill ranking of all of us, so I was the last American to start. Because the racers were running so quickly, I didn't know how my teammates had fared. The fog made everything seem especially quiet. Every twenty five seconds, a series of high pitched beeps counted down from five to one, and a racer exploded out of the start shack, skating and poling wildly, edges rasping against the ice, and disappeared into the fog. A minute after Anna started, Sean brought me the radio. Sepp's voice came over it:

"Ja, Olivia. Use your head, eh? The fog, it's not so bad after the top flat. In the tuna turn, ski a high line. Get your direction change made before the gate and stay above the compression. Stand high, give your legs some room. Then you cruise right through the ruts no problem and are in good position for the chump." By Sepp's tone of voice I assumed Anna had done the opposite—tried to run too straight and fast into one or both of the turns and then been pushed to the bottom of the compression. That was her style, her trademark—all or nothing. Sometimes it worked and sometimes... At least the racers kept leaving the gate, so she must have made it through, though without any speed. As my turn approached, I tried to focus only on what Lucy had said about skiing smart up above and on how Sepp had told me to ski his section. I tried not to think of the fog and the fear and the long line of orange fencing waiting for its catch. When the timer beeped down for me, I pushed out with all my might and called up my best Braille, trusting that Sepp was right and I'd emerge from the fog any second.

Some runs are so perfect they are etched in memory, and others are such a chaotic blur you can't remember them. This was the latter. I do know that I did exactly what Sepp said, and that when I landed from the second jump Lucy's advice miraculously popped into my head, urging me to drop into the lowest tuck I could, let my skis run as straight as possible and hang on for dear life. When I crossed the finish line, I didn't turn quickly enough to see my time before it disappeared from the scoreboard. All of my teammates were huddled somewhere out of the storm no doubt. The only American I recognized was Howard, standing like a light blue lamppost under a huge umbrella. He waved me under it and put his arm around my shoulder. Smiling down on me he said:

"Well Olivia. I think you'd better call home today."

When I finally found a results sheet, I discovered I'd actually qualified in the third spot, ahead of Jan, a B-team girl who got the final spot. Anna didn't qualify and had disappeared. In my first month as a World Cup downhiller, I was going to race in the World Championships. I stared at the wet, pulpy sheet in my hands and smiled a congratulations to myself.

I took my time getting back to the room. I expected Anna would be on her bed in our room, tuned out to her Walkman, and I wondered what I'd say to her. I found myself dreading turning the key in the lock. But when I opened the door, she was already showered and changed, with her trademark bow in place. She looked fresh, even cheerful.

"Hey—nice run today."

"Thanks." The air in the room waited for something else, but neither of us could think of anything to say. Anna was the first to speak and shifted off our non-topic.

"Hurry up so we can meet up with the guys. We're all going to get pizza and stake out a good spot at the awards plaza to watch the draw." The public bib draw was where the top 15 athletes in the next day's competition drew their starting numbers amidst fans and fanfare. With each team now pared to only four racers, Lucy would be in the draw.

"Are you ok?" I asked. For the first time in two days, Anna looked straight at me.

"Yeah. I'm fine. I'm mad at myself, and I'm not very happy. But I'm happy for you. Really." She smiled. "Now get your butt ready. We're meeting in the lobby in fifteen minutes." As she brushed past me and out the door, I smelled her flowery perfume. "Frangiapangi" or something. You could always count on boys to snap Anna out of a funk.

The next night, as promised, the storm cleared. The following morning, on my last trip to the top of the course, the Alps once again made a spectacular backdrop. I limbered up in the sunny starting area at the top of the mountain, rotating my arms in giant arcs then swinging each leg in turn. Legions of fans, many with the Swiss red cross painted on their cheeks, and most toting giant cowbells, had hiked up the mountain and now lined the course until it plunged out of sight. Periodically they broke into a chorus of "Hopp Schwiiz! Hopp Schwiiz!" practicing for the cheer that would follow each Swiss racer down the entire run.

My head was remarkably clear. I knew I was supposed

to believe I could win, to banish any other outcome from my mind. In the world according to Ken, that's how winners are made. But I couldn't get myself there. Results mattered, and they proved that it wasn't my time...yet. Still, standing there amongst the fastest women in the world, beyond the reporters and the fans and the sponsors, I felt a sort of peace, like I'd won something already. I remembered what Gus had said. Patience. It's all I needed. It's all we needed, as a team. But patience takes its own kind of discipline, and I could only hope that someone leading our team had it.

Dr. Richmond, the team doctor who pieced us all back together entirely too often, wandered over. He smiled widely and put his arm around my shoulders. The good doctor showed up at every big event, not to march around in a fancy new uniform or to socialize around the bar, but to see the rewards of his handiwork and to assure that, at least here, we'd have the best care in the world. It was Dr. Richmond who had insisted I not run downhill for a year, to slow down and let my body heal. He didn't have any agenda when he made the decision, wasn't trying to test my resolve. He just knew it was the right thing to do. He had forced patience on me when nobody else had the nerve. And it had worked. Seeing him here at the start of the World Championships, and not on a rolling chair in his office explaining my latest x-rays, reminded me of how far I'd come.

"See? I always knew you could do it." He looked down and gave my shoulder a bear-like squeeze. I felt like I was standing on top of the world in every way. Part of me wanted to stop the clock, to wrap myself in this moment and hold on to it forever because, after this run, everything would change. Whatever happened, I would no longer be an unknown, no longer be content with just making a team or moving up a list. This was the first step on a final ascent, and I had one year to plant my flag in the summit. In the background, the timer beeped as if announcing that the countdown had officially begun. Whatever lay in front of me—bring it on!

Chapter 4:
Going Downhill Fast

"Oh well. Back to reality." Anna sighed.

She walked through the door and heaved her bag on the low bed—two twin beds mooshed together—that we would be sharing. Past our bed was another bed just like it for two more roommates. Beyond that bed was a fold-out couch for a fifth person and a door to a little porch. It was more of an outdoor shelf than a porch, and it hung over a narrow alley that couldn't have been more than 10 feet wide. The ever-shadowed stucco walls of the building across the alley made up our entire view. We could see our breath in the room, and I figured it was because, as often happens in Italy, the hotel owners turned the heat off during the day.

"At least we know the food will be good." The Italian hotels we stayed in on the Europa Cup circuit weren't known for their luxurious rooms, but the food was a different story. Even the humblest inn had incredible food and lots of it, which usually made up for the tight quarters.

Anna and I took the best bed, closest to the

bathroom, and quickly unpacked the bare minimum we'd need for the next five days. There were four more technical World Cup races in Europe right after the championships, but there were no speed events until the tour's final stop in Vail. Before heading home all of us— except Lucy who used her seniority and a urinary tract infection the coaches didn't dare ask her about to negotiate an extra week at home—would race this one Europa Cup downhill in Italy. We would be joined by everyone who had not qualified for the World Championships and who were returning from two weeks on what they not so fondly called the "Balkan Tour." Normally the Europa Cup circuit doesn't stray far from the Alps of France, Switzerland, Austria, Italy and Germany. This year, however, the Eastern European skiing federations wanted to showcase their ski areas and offered to pay all the expenses of any national team racers that would attend their races. Ken loved all things free, so instead of sending the American athletes home to rest before the busy push of spring races in the States, he sent them on an all-expense-paid trip to various gray areas in Bulgaria, Romania and Yugoslavia.

We knew the Balkan travelers had arrived when Ella burst through the door and immediately went into the bathroom. "Toilet paper!" she exclaimed. "And a toilet!" Only then did she come all the way into the room and notice us.

"Hey guys." She greeted us with slightly less enthusiasm than she had shown for the toilet paper, but I wasn't offended. I knew Ella well enough to trust she'd be back to her old self once she settled in. She hurried over to claim the pullout couch with her backpack just before Greta came in the room with her big duffel bag. The normally pixie-cute Greta looked as ragged as I had ever seen her, with dark circles under her eyes and greasy hair that clumped together in dark blond ropes down her head. Her skin, normally pink and healthy, was the sickly pale blue of nonfat milk. Two weeks in the murky foothills of Eastern Europe and a diet without fresh fruit or vegetables will apparently do that. Greta spotted the open bed with relief and dropped her bag on it.

We said "hi" to Greta, but "how are you" seemed a little inappropriate considering her bedraggled appearance. Anna quickly turned the topic to our surroundings. "God it's cold in here," she announced.

"It's warmer than the van," Ella countered. The team rented Volkswagen vans that took so long to heat up that the breath from 8 passengers condensed into tiny icicles on the uninsulated metal roof. If and when it did warm up, like in a long European Autobahn tunnel, the icicles on the roof then melted back down onto the passengers so that they were cold *and* damp.

"And warmer than the hotel in Bulgaria," Greta added. It didn't take long for details of their trip to emerge. Ella described dirty hotels with bathrooms that consisted merely of a showerhead and a single drain down which all water and waste went, dustbunnies so thick that everyone wore her shoes right to bed, and mystery meat that made the horsemeat casseroles in France sound like five star feasts.

This was not the time to tell them about our spacious hotel room in Switzerland, about powder skiing in Verbier before the races, about taking a helicopter across the valley for an afternoon training session on uncrowded slopes, or about dancing with the boys in the hotel disco. I stole a look at Anna, and our eyes agreed to a vow of silence.

Partway through the description, Greta, who appeared to still be in shell shock, got up to take a shower.

"Finally!" Ella said under her breath. When we heard the shower water running, Ella told us how Greta had gone tilt at the living conditions. "She was so grossed out by the bathrooms and the floors that she didn't take one shower the entire time." That explained the hair. "And she refused to eat anything but dry cereal." That explained the exceptional pallor. Greta was an only child who had gone straight from her overly attentive parents to a ski academy to the US Ski Team on a pre-ordained path. Somebody was always taking care of her, and she had no idea how to fend for herself. All the talent in the world—and she had plenty—couldn't offset her crippling dependence on those around her. Not yet at least.

While Greta was in the shower the door opened again. A tall girl, more of a woman really, filled the doorway, an enormous red and blue US Ski Team duffel bag slung over her shoulder. She brushed away the wavy swath of thick blonde hair that had escaped from her ponytail and huffed across the room in three steps, dropping her bag on Greta's bed. She picked up Greta's bag and dropped it on the floor, then proceeded to unpack two small speakers and a massive collection of cassette tapes, which she then arranged neatly along the entire length of the headboard.

Jan was on the "B" team, a rung above me on the US Ski Team ladder but, as far as Ken was concerned, she had been there too long. She had qualified behind me for the final spot in the World Championships downhill. That, however, was not considered a victory. Instead of congratulations, Ken had given her an ultimatum. If she didn't get a top 3 at this Europa Cup or a top 10 at the final World Cup in Vail, she was off the team. Jan didn't confide in any of us. We only knew this because Sean—a shameless gossip—had overheard a conversation between the reps—equally shameless gossips—in the ski room.

Jan had made the four hour drive from Crans Montana to this small Italian resort with "her" rep, a guy named Scott who prepared skis for the company that sponsored Jan. Jan had entered what we called the "cash in/fade out" phase of her career. Not on purpose of course. Cash in/fade out was rarely deliberate. You didn't actually sign a contract that you suspected could be the nail in the coffin of your career. She had signed a contract with a ski company that offered her a lot of money to use their somewhat questionable skis, and she probably thought it was a good move. She would get her own rep and her pick of the company's best skis. They would put her on posters and postcards and use her in all their brochures. They would make her their star.

The only problem was that if the skis (or boots) weren't just right for the athlete, she might be washed up in just one season. A coach who cared about an athlete recognized and counseled against potential cash in/fade out decisions. Sepp certainly would have if he had joined our team in time, before she'd signed the papers. But the US Ski Team had been hastening her departure for years, ever since they had kept her off the 1984 Olympic team.

Then, at 21, Jan was the third best downhiller in the country but Ken's predecessor, the Big Cheese at the time, had decided to only take two men and two women downhillers to Sarajevo. At 24 Jan could just now be coming in to her prime, and on any other team she might have been. But after two years of being ignored by the coaches and then this past year of skiing on crap skis, she was considered over the hill. At least having her own rep meant she had someone to talk to, someone who we all suspected was also her boyfriend. Athlete/rep relationships weren't really supposed to happen, but they weren't as taboo as athlete/coach relationships, both of which happened often enough. Considering Jan's age it wasn't really anyone's business whenever she and Scott took off on their own, and showed up at the next venue hours later than expected.

This time, however, showing up late meant Jan had to share a bed with Greta. The aging vet and the clueless rookie did not mix well. When Greta emerged from the shower, Jan figured out whose bag she'd moved. With undisguised contempt, she look up at the ceiling, as if she might ignite two holes in it with her eyes.

"Great. Just freaking great." She let out a loud sigh and left the room.

By dinnertime, when we were all digging in to our Euro style personal pizzas, Ella was back to herself, entertaining us with stories from the Balkan Tour. She was eighteen, the same age as Greta, but she was more of a workhorse than a thoroughbred. She didn't have Greta's perfect body and textbook technique. She was bigger, more like all the European skiers her age and not at all like the Barbie physique Ken prized. But Ella knew how to let her skis run and make the most of momentum. Her runs weren't always pretty but they were often fast.

"Hey, did you hear what happened to us on our way to the races just outside of Graz?" Ella recounted what was by far the finest moment of their trip. Their van had just turned off the autobahn and was driving on a slushy side road when the traffic ahead suddenly came to a dead standstill and people started rushing out of their cars.

"Trent told us to stay in the van so, of course, we all got out. There was a truck overturned down the embankment and purple stuff lying all over the snow. Get this—it was a Milka chocolate truck!" Our eyes widened as she described the scene.

"People were everywhere, scrambling down the snow bank in their little black shoes, filling their coat pockets, shopping bags, backpacks, hats—anything they could find in their cars. The driver didn't even bother to try stopping them. It was like the best Easter Egg hunt ever!"

Just as she was telling us how much chocolate they had all squirreled away, the Europa Cup downhill coach Trent came by our table on his way to the restroom. Trent was one of Ken's best friends, and that—certainly not his talent for coaching women—was probably why he had the job. He looked like he had walked right out of a deodorant commercial, with slicked back hair and an overly tight turtleneck that displayed his pumped-up chest. He loved manly things like football, cowboy boots, chewing tobacco, and of course, pretty little women.

"Can't stop talking about the chocolate again, huh Ella?" He chuckled as he stopped at our table. "Are you sure you really need all of that?" Trent eyed the surviving half of Ella's pizza.

Ella put down her fork and knife and let her shoulders drop as she exhaled and glared at Trent. Across the table Greta, who had already wolfed down her entire pizza, immediately perked up.

"If you're not going to finish that I will. I'm starving!"

Trent pretended not to hear Greta and fixed his eyes on Ella's, daring her with a tsk-tsking smirk across his face.

"Well? Do you want it or not?" pressed Greta, who had come over with her empty plate.

"I guess not." Quick as a snake's tongue, Greta's fork speared the half pizza then retracted it to her plate. "Mmmmm!" she purred, retreating with her prize.

Back in the room, Anna, Ella and I hung out while Greta was in the lobby calling home. Ella was back in her funk. She told us how Trent took every opportunity to hint that she needed to lose weight, though he never said it outright. Ella was one of the fastest skiers on the Europa Cup team. She hovered at the edge of the top 15 —the best American on most days—but not impressive enough for Trent who was eager to deliver the next downhill star.

"He called me zaftig right before the start one day," Ella explained. "Zaftig! How is that supposed to make me ski faster?"

I cringed momentarily then smiled.

"Are you sure he didn't just get one of those "Word a Day" calendars for Christmas?"

Ella smiled the slightest bit while tearing open the lavender wrapper of a Milka chocolate bar. I felt for Ella, especially when it came to the chocolate. I never had an issue with Milka, but boy did I ever suffer through a fateful love affair with Ritter Sport chocolate bars. When I was 16 and traveling through Europe alone, I must have downed one of those 100-gram bars every day, until none of my clothes fit. Thinking back on it made me glad not to have been anywhere near that overturned truck. Ella continued to vent.

"For some reason, it's fine for Greta to finish in the Thirties and 'get experience,' but he keeps giving me ultimatums, saying this is my last trip to Europe unless I start skiing faster—as if I'm *trying* to suck. I feel like he has it in for me."

It was odd how the coaches worshipped the as-yet unproven Greta. Just one year earlier, after I had fallen in a slalom in Germany, Ken, who was frustrated from a month of our bad results on the Europa Cup, read me the riot act right on the side of the course. He claimed I'd tried to fall and lectured me on all the things that separated me from a "real champion."

"Real champions never give up. When they start something they finish it. Real champions want to win every time they get into the starting gate. They're first on the hill and last off. Real champions don't complain when the conditions aren't perfect…"

I endured his rant by composing a speech in my head about "real coaches" who know the difference between pushing hard and beating a dead horse. But I kept quiet and listened. I started to feel the tiniest bit like a complete failure until he fixed his angry eyes on me for his final zinger.

"A real champion wouldn't have given up like that. *Greta* wouldn't have fallen."

The closing line didn't make me think any worse of Greta. But it made me wonder how Ken had ever gotten, much less kept, his job. How many real champions had Ken and Trent and all the coaches overlooked while waiting for their precious, perfect Gretas to pan out. And, why wasn't the best they had ever good enough?

While pondering this I must have been staring at Ella as she broke another chunk off the Milka Bar because she suddenly became defensive.

"I know! This isn't helping. But the more I think

about my weight, and the more Trent harps on me about it, the more chocolate I end up eating."

The duffel bag pocket brimming with chocolate bars wasn't really a good long-term solution for Ella, but it seemed to give her some comfort because a tinge of relief crept into her voice when she said: "Well, at least I'm not Jan."

"Where is Jan anyway?" I realized I had not seen her at dinner.

"Out." The word hung in the air, because of the depth of its meaning.

In the days that followed, just before every training run we gathered at the top of the course and checked in with the coaches on the radio. They made their comments: either things to improve from the run before, new things to try or a report on course conditions. Each of us held the radio to our ears in turn and listened to our specific instructions:

"Delay your turn on the first gate of the corridor so that you can come under the second gate and have better direction over the bump...Your hands are drifting back. As you go over the bump pull up your feet and push your hands and hips forward... try to get back in your tuck quicker on the last pitch..." They always had a few things for each of us to work on. Every time Jan checked in, they simply said, "Course clear!" indicating that she was free to go, in every sense.

For her part, Jan seemed to have accepted her fate. It was hard to believe this was the same person who, upon our first meeting, had shattered my illusions of what a World Cup ski racer was like. I was 15 and staying by special invitation with the US Ski Team girls at the National Championships Downhill. The morning of the downhill race, after an early jog, a stretch and my healthy breakfast of oatmeal and herbal tea, I was dressed and headed out the door with all my gear. Jan—already an Amazonian presence at nineteen—emerged from her room in our condo, loped across the living room and casually wolfed down two bowls of Capt'n Crunch. I stifled a laugh, not only at her nutritional choice but at the fact that, given her lateness, she'd barely have time to digest that junk. Two hours later, Jan became our National Downhill Champion.

Two years later, I roomed with her again at my first European US Ski Team training camp. She was in her punk rock phase with close-cropped hair dyed Joan Jett black to match all her clothing. The look alone was intimidating enough to a rookie but, just for good measure, she yelled at me for taking a nap on my first afternoon ("I am NOT going to stay up all night listening to you toss and turn!"). When her soon-to-be ex-boyfriend called desperately trying to track her down, she knew it was him and made me answer the phone. As soon as I picked up Jan called out loudly:

"If it's Derek I'm not here."

I looked at the phone.

"Uh. She's not here." Pause. I covered the receiver and whispered to Jan, "He can hear you."

"Tell him to move his stuff out. He can take the knives and plates, but the candlesticks and the stereo are mine."

"Uh, don't take the candlesti…You heard that, huh? Yeah, maybe if you called back in the morning that'd be better. Sure, I'll tell her. Uh, maybe you should tell her that one yourself."

Auf wiedersehen Derek.

The two of us had never been warm and fuzzy together but, I think, finally, Jan respected me. And being around her and Greta together, I started to understand her bitterness at the whole natural order of things, where younger skiers keep prodding you, wearing you down and threatening to steal your spot at your first sign of weakness.

That process was prematurely accelerated by the US Ski Team—by the Kens and Trents and Phils who were far too common and whose relentless quest for the next young sensation ran completely counter to Gus's philosophy of patience. I suspected that had something to do with why the Swiss were whooping up on us so badly. If Greta "made it" (and she was being given every chance to do just that), would it be because of her talent or because she had so many opportunities and so many people believing in her? Likewise, if the coaches succeeded in making someone as talented as Jan fail, who really won?

When I came into the room after the first day of training, I noticed the unmistakable odor of fried electrical matter. Greta was standing there, looking at the blow-dryer she held in her hands. Jan's blow-dryer.

"You blew it up?"

"I couldn't have. I mean it shouldn't have. I put the little thingie on, see? She held up the end of the cord with a gray plastic pronged attachment on the end.

"That's the adapter. *This* is the converter." I held up a black boxy thing lying next to the power outlet. "If you don't put this on before the adapter it's sort of like lighting a birthday candle with a flamethrower."

"Oh." Her face went completely red, and it looked

like she might cry. I actually felt sorry for her. She still needed full time care. I wasn't going to be it, but I did want to make her feel better.

"It's ok. Everyone does it…once."

"Jan's going to kill me." She was probably right.

Just then, the door opened and Greta darted into the bathroom. She relaxed when she saw it was only Anna.

"Whoa. Holy burning plastic. What blew up?"

"Jan's blow-dryer," Greta and I answered in unison. Anna was unconcerned and offered her usual assessment.

"She'll get over it in a week."

Still, Greta was terrified. I offered to be the one to tell Jan if Greta promised to buy her a new blow-dryer when we got back to the States. Fortunately we only had a few days left, and Anna had a blow-dryer that she said she'd let Jan use.

"Just don't touch her speakers, "Anna advised. "If you blow those up you're on your own."

On race day we were all so excited to get home that it felt like we had one foot on the plane already. It was a relatively easy downhill, which made me focus all the more because of the first (and possibly best) downhill advice I'd ever gotten. When I was 13 years old and just discovering the combined effects that a one-piece speed suit, long skis and peer pressure have on velocity, the full-time cowboy, who was my part-time coach, shared his valuable wisdom: "A wild horse will hurt you, but a tame horse will kill you." He meant that you had to respect every course and never let your guard down, especially on the easy ones. Once you lose that respect, you're toast.

At the end of the day Anna finished in 2nd place and I finished 3rd. For both of us, it was our best Europa Cup finish ever, and Anna felt redeemed for failing to qualify at the Worlds. Jan had a good race too, but finished 5th, just beneath Trent's bar. She disappeared before the awards ceremony and, by the time we got back to the room, she was already packed up and headed to the Zurich airport with Scott.

Chapter 5:
Rocky Mountain High

Thank God for Vail. Well, maybe not God exactly but the owner of Vail, who, as far as we were concerned, was close enough. By the time we made it from Zurich, through Customs in Boston, to Denver and finally chugged over the Vail pass two hours later, we were exhausted. But once we stepped out of the vans and into the welcoming arms of the Vail Valley, it was as if a blast of Rocky Mountain air erased a season's worth of fatigue.

For years already, Colorado had felt like a second home. The ski world convenes in Colorado for early season skiing and, every year since I was 15, I had gone there for either a training camp in November, national championships in January, a Junior Olympics in March or all of the above. My sisters were both students at the University of Colorado during those years, so I always got to see them on my trips, even if only for ice cream in the Denver airport. Sometimes, when I had a day or two off between races, I would hitch a ride to visit them in Boulder. From my point of view as the party mascot, college life—friends and boyfriends filtering through at all hours—looked exciting, even enticing. Someday it would be fun to be normal like that.

College and Colorado were connected in my mind from my very first trip to the Rockies which happened to be to Vail. Back then I only knew Vail as the place President Gerald Ford skied. The clips I'd seen of him gently ambling down the slopes, flanked by secret service agents, made me think it was far too tame to be any fun. Colorado just seemed cold and dry. But when I got invited to a US Ski Team camp that year, I discovered the real Vail. Squaw Valley, with its rugged beauty and crazy characters, would always be my favorite place to ski. But Vail was paradise, a snow-globe-like world almost too good to be true.

The slopes were perfectly manicured, except on the powder days when the steeper ones were left untouched so that we could float through knee high fluff, as light and perfect as that powder I remembered in Jackson Hole. Every day of that first camp, it seemed, was a powder day, where the only sounds on the mountain were the "flump" of snow falling off trees as we brushed by them, the distant thud of avalanche bombs thrown by the ski patrol and our own laughter. It felt just like home, which put me totally at ease with my mostly eastern competition. The coaches were not pleased that training and high pressure time trials were replaced with powder and tree skiing, but the rest of us were thrilled. We were no longer easterners and westerners, downhillers or tech skiers. We were just a bunch of kids skiing ourselves silly in a ton of snow, building jumps, doing stupid tricks and getting snow down our necks. In one way, however, I was unlike the other kids, which is why my sisters swooped in one day to kidnap me from camp.

Laura and Eliza arrived in Eliza's rattly neon yellow Renault and took me from Vail to Leadville. At 19 and nearly 21, Laura and Eliza were practically grown-ups and temporarily assumed the role of parents for this occasion. We spent a freezing night in the cheapest motel available, then went to a diner the next morning where Eliza insisted we splurge on a huge omelet for me.

"You need brain food," she asserted.

"Well, I need coffee," said Laura, whose college schedule did not involve early mornings. "This is way too early to eat."

The rest of the kids my age at camp were high school sophomores, but I was a senior set to graduate in January, so I had to take my SAT tests. And, I had to take them in a strange town with a bunch of strangers. Skiing fast was critical for my Plan A, becoming a famous ski racer, but good SAT scores were critical for my Plan B, getting in to a good college. My sisters delivered me to Leadville High School with two number 2 pencils and my passport for identification because I was still too young for a driver's license.

"Good luck!" Laura gave me a hug. "Don't worry. You always test well, and you'll ace the essay." Eliza saluted: "See you on the other side!"

Three hours later, I emerged from the back of the fluorescently lit gym into the blinding winter sunlight. The heavy door closed slowly behind me then clicked shut decisively as if to say, "High school. Check!"

Much had changed in the five years since that first trip to Vail. Gerald Ford had a lot more vacation time, Vail had become a regular stop on the World Cup tour and my sisters were well out of college, working for a living in the "real world." I, however, was still in my would-be dream world, though far from the fame of my Plan A fantasy. As for Plan B, I had yet to enroll in college full-time and was beginning to wonder if I ever would. That what-the-hell-am-I-doing-with-my-life anxiety, the thing that boiled inside during the darkest moments of winter, simmered harmlessly on the backburner when we were in Vail. Coming here was the closest we came to knowing what it was like to be a European, racing every weekend amongst fans and friends and having a legitimate career.

Throngs of friendly locals, aspiring ski racers and fired-up spectators high-fived us as we glided past them in the liftline and broke into frequent chants of "U.S.A." at all hours. They didn't wear yak suits and paint their faces, but we felt the love nonetheless. Walking down Vail's main drag, Bridge Street, past its busy shops, restaurants and bars, felt like moving through one big block party, this time in our own neighborhood. Every night a different restaurant hosted our entire team for elaborate dinners. In addition to the fans and what seemed like everyone we'd ever met in the ski business, we all had a contingent of friends and family we looked forward to seeing. And there was the boyfriend brigade which, as usual, didn't directly affect me. Indirectly though, boyfriends put girlfriends in a much better mood, which was nice.

Vail's owner had deep pockets and a soft spot for our team. He used them both to make sure we had every advantage on our home turf. The mountain closed off the race hill so that we could train on it a week before the other teams rolled into town, just like the Europeans did on their home courses. We stayed in deluxe condos and had the run of plush athletic facilities with weight rooms, pools and indoor tennis courts, a far cry from the dim, dusty, unheated, elementary school gyms we used in Europe. "Mexican food!" "Sushi!" "Slurpees!" "Real showers!" Each of us had something we especially craved after a winter of too much cabbage and mystery meat, and all of it was at our fingertips in Vail.

On the evening we arrived, Vail's owner took one look at our group in our dingy light blue uniforms, stained with a winter's worth of chairlift grease and van dirt, and made a request:

"Give me all your clothes."

By 6:30 am the next day, several ski area employees were at our doors, bearing armloads of freshly cleaned uniforms.

Anna looked at the pile of clothes, which the rest of the girls were delightedly freeing from the plastic bags, and at the remains of the giant welcome fruit basket that stood on the coffee table, still brimming with snacks.

"Treat a man as he is and he will remain as he is. Treat a man as he can and should be, and he will become as he can and should be."

"Goethe? Emerson?" I loved quotations, but could never keep their origins straight.

"Nah." She nodded at the steaming mug in her hand. "Tea bag. But whoever did say it was on to something."

Instead of making us feel like inexperienced rookies or reserving special treatment for the A Team, Vail treated everyone of us like the rock stars we hoped someday to be. It was remarkable how radically the group's mood changed when each individual felt a whiff of respect. Vail was our last chance to end the season on a good note. If there was anywhere we could muster confidence and a semblance of pride it was here, where the tea bag wisdom was working its magic.

If ever anyone thrived on the extra attention it was Lucy. A born performer, she raised her game exponentially when placed in a starring role, working the crowd at every turn, from the liftlines to the local ski shops to the restaurants where we were spoiled every night. Lucy was such a human study that even the prospect of rooming with her didn't bother me, much. But it was somewhat torturous to hear her phone conversations, planning her upcoming trip to "The Islands" with her boyfriend and "agonizing" about negotiating her Olympic year contracts.

Her agent—a guy who embraced hair gel and the blazer-over-t-shirt-and-jeans look—showed up at big events and smiled when he shook your hand, while simultaneously looking over your shoulder for someone he really wanted to talk to. He had just scored a big headgear sponsor for Lucy. That meant that in addition to the enviable "retainer" checks she'd be getting from her ski equipment sponsors, she'd also get a much bigger check to wear the "*Burst*" name and logo on her helmet.

Burst was a new energy bar on the market that relied on sports personalities to promote their name specifically and the concept of energy bars in general. So far most energy bars we'd tried had the taste and consistency of glue. The only way we could actually eat them while training was to keep them in our racing suits where body heat kept them pliable. (They did come in handy as soccer shin guards though.) In addition to paying her directly, *Burst* would also be using her in their national ad campaign, in print and on TV, giving her other sponsors more visibility. And, of course, she'd get more *Burst* bars than she could ever eat, at least on one set of teeth. It was win, win, win...as long as she won.

Most of us felt lucky just to have our training and travel expenses paid with a little money to spend in the off-season, which made Lucy's constant chatter about sponsors and contracts all the more offensive.

"Do you have to be a jerk to win?" Anna wondered out loud while she was in our room during one of Lucy's extra loud phone conversations with her agent. I didn't answer, not for fear of being overheard, but because I really didn't know the answer.

Except for Natalie's bronze medal in the Combined event, the US Ski Team had pretty much bombed at the World Championships. We had quit going to the nightly awards ceremonies and fireworks displays because we tired of hearing the Swiss national anthem. Their men and women won eight of the ten events. In the races that followed, it was clear that the success of the big stars had infected their entire team. Now even the middle tier Swiss athletes were magically popping on to the podium like marmots appearing from beneath rocks on a sunny day. The opposite was happening with our team. Whatever personal successes we had—me qualifying for the World's, Anna's Europa Cup result, Lucy's early season win—got swallowed by the team's general downward spiral.

Ever since joining the US Ski Team, my primary form of motivation had been challenge rather than encouragement. I felt like I had to apologize for what I wasn't rather than look forward to what I hoped to become. Athletes like Donna and Natalie were so good so young that, like cream, they seemed to simply rise to the top. Unfortunately, they were seen as the norm. The rest of us making steady progress were seen as the disappointing exceptions.

Dan and Sepp didn't share that mentality. Like Gus, they preached patience but, by the time they came on board to save us, much irreversible damage had been done. The entire tier of B team athletes—a generation of skiers who where supposed to take over after the Sarajevo Olympics—had been driven out. Only Jan remained, and she was on life support. The rest of us on the C team had come up through the ranks with Ken or Trent who focused their awareness and ours on our flaws. For many of us, like Anna and Ella and me, those feelings of inadequacy centered on our bodies. The one sturdily-built person on the team who embraced her physique (and there probably was only one) was Lucy. I learned that the hard way after our first day of training in Vail, when she emerged from the shower into our bedroom.

"Look at me!" Lucy said, more to herself than to me I hoped. She stood there naked, facing the full-length mirror on the back of the open bathroom door, a handful of belly fat clutched in each fist. She smiled back at her image. This was certainly a new twist on her narcissism. I could only stare and could not stop doing that. I couldn't even look at myself in that way without flinching. And yet, at her invitation, I found myself transfixed. The image certainly didn't entice me, but her attitude—like everything else about Lucy—commanded my attention then held it there.

In a normal roommate situation, this would be an ideal time to exit or at least become engrossed in my book, tune out to my Walkman or go for a walk. But I couldn't figure out if I wanted to leave the room or clap. It had been six years since what dear brother Jamie called my "refugee phase," six years since I had lost 25 pounds in two months and reveled in the power of plummeting to

94 pounds, six years since Blake, the first US Ski Team boy who called me by name and the one I worshipped, had asked me if I'd rather be thin or fast and I had chosen fast. Six years later, even though I never regretted that decision, I still loathed my body most days. The coaches made no secret that they wanted long and lean. *I* wanted long and lean. Even though, eventually, the coaches and I had accepted the reality of my less than perfect body, I would always be ashamed of *my* rolls.

Yet here was Lucy celebrating, even embracing, literally, her rolls. Part of her pleasure came from the feeling of vindication. I had gotten subtle hints and comments about my weight from coaches along the way, especially from Jeff, the hard core trainer and Marine. "G.I. Jeff," as we called him, often looked me up and down in my shorts and t-shirt, shaking his head disapprovingly at my general thickness. But he told Lucy outright that she was overweight and out of shape.

Lucy even got kicked off the team at one point for being "unfit." It was after she returned from her exile (quite tanned and fully refreshed) that she started winning races on the Europa Cup. The faster she skied, the more weight she gained, and with every good result she earned immunity from the coaches. She had the freedom to give her body exactly what it needed while the rest of us had to justify our choices, however reasonable.

Considering our sport, it stands to reason that a ski racer's chief attribute is toughness. You need it to stay out in the elements for hours in sub-zero temperatures; you need it to hammer your arms and legs against hundreds of plastic gates every training day; you need it to push your body down steep icy courses at speeds in excess of 70 miles per hour; you need it to survive the inevitable body-bashing crashes at those speeds; and you need it to dust yourself off and get up to speed again.

Strangely, coaches like Ken and Trent had never seen (or admitted) the connection between weight and performance, or the simple reality that nothing about our sport favors fragility. But Lucy breathed the fire beneath that truth. When Lucy dropped in to her tuck on course you could almost hear her skis shift into overdrive, and see her become a freight train with no brakes, an unstoppable force. Even off the hill she exuded power and strength. I envied this confidence that was taking her into a different realm.

That small piece of respect, and sheer shock, kept me from leaving our room as Lucy turned and looked at herself from every angle, flexing and grabbing her thighs to test their strength. Finally she squared up to the mirror, bent her elbows and knees, made both hands in to a fist and brought them together in front of her hips in a half crab pose.

"Grrrrr!"

We had a downhill and a Super G in Vail. Because the downhill course is relatively flat on the top half—a "glider's" course as opposed to a "technical" course with lots of steep turns—weather, ski preparation, snow conditions and luck often play a bigger than usual role on race day. For once, all those things seemed to be on our team's side. In the first race, a blanket of clouds caused poor visibility for the early racers. Minutes before Lucy left the start gate, the clouds parted and the track warmed up and "glazed." That is, the path worn by the previous skiers shone with a film of water. Then, as she pushed out of the gate, a thin cloud covered the sun and the temperature dropped slightly, just enough for the glaze to freeze into a slick, fast surface. Lucy blasted out of the start with her usual confidence and rode that enchanted trail right into first place. The sun came out after her run, slowing the track and preventing nearly everyone else from getting close. Nearly everyone. Forty racers later, another cloud covered the sun, causing the track to freeze, and this time it was Greta's turn to ride the shiny path to glory. For her, that meant 15th place—her first World Cup point (points were awarded to the top 15 spots)—and her ticket to the World Cup downhill team. The next day Lucy won again, this time on sheer momentum.

I finished in the top 20 both days, which wasn't so bad, and I was definitely closing the gap. Three seconds off the winner's pace was still an eternity but it was much better than five. Considering Greta's and Lucy's success, however, I hardly felt like celebrating. Back in our room Lucy fielded calls from the *New York Times* and *Sports Illustrated*.

In a normal year, the mainstream press might not have noticed the race but, with the Olympics less than a year away, everyone wanted the "inside" story. How did Lucy "come from nowhere" to win two World Cups in two days. Of course, nobody comes from nowhere. Every breakthrough involves a little luck and a lot of preparation. Lucy deserved what she had gotten, but still I burned with jealousy. This whiff of possibility—the knowledge that if *she* could do it, *I* could certainly do it—only filled me with regret. Why had it taken someone else's success and why had it taken until the end of the season to believe in myself? My mind grumbled over that as I leaned on my ski poles and looked back up at the hill after the Super G, my final World Cup of the season.

I was in that position when Dan made his way down to the finish area after the race was done. He came over to where I stood. Despite Lucy's and Greta's flurry of success, Dan still appeared to be dragging under a season's worth of disappointment. As usual though, he mustered some enthusiasm when he saw me and tried to refocus on what I'd done right. After all, Sepp would be sure to tell me what I'd done wrong.

"You were great in the middle section. We'll have to look at the split times, but I'll bet you were in the top 10 through there." I sighed and held my gaze up the hill.

"What's the matter?"

"I want a do-over. Split times, training runs, the middle section. When is it all going to come together? I feel so... *lame*."

Normally when I got down on myself, Dan would remind me of how far I'd come in a short time, how it takes time and consistency to be great and that by missing two straight years with injuries and then having three different sets of coaches I hadn't had much of either. Like Gus, he'd point out that the Swiss—not just the athletes but their coaches and the reps—had been together for a long time, and how that (not some mystical talent), explained their success. He would convince me not to be so hard on myself. *Normally* that's what he'd do. But not today. When he spoke, his voice was hard, his look blatantly exasperated.

"That's your problem right there! You have to believe in yourself or nobody else will. Look at Lucy. Technically and physically she's got nothing on you. But she *thinks* she's better than you, and everyone else. That's the difference."

"Tell me about it." I didn't mean to change the

subject, but my mind flashed on the still-fresh image of Lucy grabbing her fat in the mirror.

"If I have to see her checking herself out in the mirror naked again I might hurl!" Even though Dan winced, I could tell he had softened a little.

"Ok, that's *way* more than I needed to know. The point is, so what if you're not Lucy? So what if you didn't win World Cups in your teens like Donna and Natalie? It hardly ever happens like that. And it doesn't happen the same way for anybody. I was there in '84—I saw those girls. Sure they were talented, but that's not what they had on you. They knew how to ask for their skis. Not just skis, you know, but everything. Just like Lucy. You have more talent than most anyone out there, but it's not enough. It'll never be enough. Trust me, talent—talent on its own—is way overrated."

Just then Rebecca skied past us, and he mumbled something that sounded like, "case in point." Perfectly, beautifully sculpted Rebecca had somehow retained a spot on the team for four years and, despite having no injuries, had progressed nowhere. She couldn't get any more perfect, technically and physically. But she still wasn't fast. Meanwhile Lucy, with her multitude of flaws, could take down everyone on her good days just because she had the audacity to believe that she deserved to. She didn't just ask for her skis. She demanded them.

"Promise me something," Dan said. "Remember how badly you feel right now. Keep this feeling, and use it all summer. Use it as a spark to ignite every single training run, imagine it as a pack of wild dogs chasing you on every sprint at the track. Use it to remind yourself that you can't just take what you get. Go after what *you* need to ski your fastest. Then, when you get into the starting gate for the first race next year, release the hounds."

Nobody had ever told me to hang on to disappointment, but it was worth a try.

After Dan left, I retrieved my parka and pants from the pile of baby blue clothes Sean had carried down from the start in an enormous bag. Then I headed towards the ski room, where the reps were already waxing and packing away all the skis. Jan was just outside the finish area, still in her skis, standing alone with her head down. She reminded me of Ginger in *Black Beauty*, the once-gleaming mare who had become a dull sway-backed workhorse, waiting to die while still hooked to the carriage. Jan wasn't the only one of her era who'd ended her skiing career like this. She was just the most stubborn and hung on the hardest. I wanted to scoot by unnoticed, but somehow it didn't seem right. Anything—even feeling disliked—is worse than feeling invisible. As I passed her I stopped, barely muttering, "Hang in there, Jan."

She looked up slowly, looking blank and exhausted, then locked on my eyes.

"They're bastards Sharpie. Don't ever forget it. They don't give a crap about you."

I felt a chill as if the Ghost of Christmas Future had just spoken. But I also felt sorry for Jan and wished she didn't have to be seen like this. I wished anyone—nutcase or not—who had committed so much to this team didn't have to leave it without a shred of dignity. Mostly, I wished it wouldn't end that way for me.

Chapter 6:
Hotel California—One great couch

Welcome to the Hotel California
Such a lovely place
Such a lovely face
Plenty of room at the Hotel California
Any time of year, you can find it here.

~Hotel California, The Eagles

Park City may be known as the official home of the US Ski Team because the administrative offices are there. But if there was an official couch of the US Ski Team in those days, it was the one in our house. "The couch" was a built-in platform topped with thick cushions that wrapped around two sides of the living room beneath a row of picture windows. The windows let in maximum sun as well as a panoramic view of the ski hill, making it a cheerful perch for skiers, unless they happened to be injured.

Unfortunately, most skiers who ended up spending a lot of time on our couch were injured. Our home in Squaw was less than an hour away from the team doctor's hospital in South Lake Tahoe, which was convenient when Jamie had his five knee surgeries and I had my two. Our home earned the name "Hotel California" because everyone on the US Ski Team who got injured seemed to stop here for a night or ten on the way to the hospital, after surgery, or both. It helped that the hotel was staffed by my mother, who cooked, cleaned, administered medications and became a surrogate mother for all guests.

None visited more frequently than Nellie. When she first arrived on our couch, I didn't exactly dislike her, but I didn't have any compelling reason to like her either. I'd known about her ever since we were both 13, and my Dad had shown me her picture in the *New York Times* magazine. He was stretched out on the famous couch on a Sunday afternoon, his Hush Puppies kicked off, reading an article that detailed the training routine at an intense ski racing academy in Vermont. Inside was a full-page picture of Nellie decked out in all the latest apparel from her sponsors, slashing through slalom gates in the frigid haze of snowmaking guns under the earnest gaze of coaches at the side of the course. Nellie Lukovic, "discovered" on her local ski hill by academy scouts, and brought to the academy on scholarship had become the poster child for elite skiing. The look of determination clearly visible through her goggle lens told all that the story didn't say outright. Ski racing was her ticket to opportunity, her chance at everything from athletic excellence to world travel to an education, and she literally raced like her life depended on it.

"Look at this girl." My Dad held up the magazine and her picture for my inspection. "She looks pretty good." My Dad wasn't one of the high-pressure parents who followed his kids down the race courses yelling "encouragement" or offering us prizes and rewards for good results. There certainly were enough of those to spare. Instead he employed the power of positive thinking with a little routine before each race. "Well, little person, what's your M.A.?" he'd ask. My automatic response was "W.A." though sometimes, when I wasn't feeling especially confident I added, "I guess." He'd complete the ritual by reciting, "If your M.A. is W.A., you're O.K." Usually I cringed when we went through this exchange about mental attitude and winning attitude, but when I saw what some other parents put their kids through I learned to appreciate his restraint.

My Dad may not have added pressure to the mix, but he wasn't above fanning our every competitive flame. When he waved the magazine in front of me I barely looked his way while giving him the "who cares" eye roll.

"Looks like she'll be giving you a run for your money someday, Little Person." With what appeared to be a smile, he got up to leave the room, first putting the magazine down on the coffee table, open to the picture of the girl who, I already knew, I wished didn't exist. I avoided the magazine like the hairballs our cat Cinders threw up periodically, circling widely around its resting spot, but finally could not resist the temptation to see her picture. In a smaller inset she looked straight at the camera, beaming, undeniably cute, with perfect olive skin, thick, shiny chestnut hair and blindingly white teeth inside a huge smile. She might be my worst nightmare.

Two years later, I actually met Nellie at a US Ski Team camp fondly referred to as "the Shootout." The dog-eat-dog elimination derby pitted 30 girls and women, ranging in age from 15 to 22, against each other to fill four spots on the team. It was the US Ski Team's version of the Circle of Life; out with the old, in with the new. I'd never wanted anything so badly: the cool uniform with my name embroidered on the sleeve; the all-expense-paid world travel; the year-round training with the best skiers in the country. Goodbye station wagons and frozen PB-Js, hello airlines and wienerschnitzel. It could all be mine in one short week.

I flailed at the camp, crumbling from both the pressure and the lack of support. None of my own coaches were there, and any of the athletes I did know were, like me, consumed by looking out for themselves. I drowned my sorrows with milkshakes and called home every few days, desperate to talk to somebody, anybody, who cared. My mom usually answered, full of cheer.

"Hi honey. How's camp?" Just hearing her voice made me choke up, like I did when I was eight years old and called, homesick, from summer camp. I felt about as mature now, telling her about how the other girls were mean and the coaches ignored me, etc, etc... It all sounded so stupid when I put it into words.

"People only pick on you when they're jealous or they feel bad about themselves. I'm sure once they get to know you..." She dispensed her standard advice, then quickly relinquished the phone to my Dad who was eager to hear all about how I stacked up against the other athletes. As usual, he tried to analyze his way through my despair.

"You can't be skiing *that* badly."

"Oh I am." I assured him.

"What are you doing wrong?"

"I don't know."

"Well what are the coaches saying to you?"

"Nothing."

"What do you mean nothing?"

"I mean *nothing*. Nothing at all!" I started to let it pour out. "That's what's so frustrating. I don't know what I'm doing wrong, but the harder I try the slower I get."

Dad saw his opportunity to score hard data and lunged for it like a shiny prize.

"So they're timing you?"

"Not yet."

"Then how do you know you're slower?"

I hated this. Trying to explain to "fact man" the nuances of a rejection that is felt but not spoken. How did I know I was slow? I could tell by the way I was being ignored.

I couldn't help being jealous of Nellie. If I felt like I was in an aimless swirl, Nellie appeared to be on a preordained path to greatness.

She was completely comfortable with all the academy coaches and athletes at the camp. The word was out about her intensity, about how she used to get up at 5 am to train in the dark before school. Elementary school. Even the US Ski Team coaches talked to her with something close to respect, and she was so unfazed by the pressure that she swished easily into the welcoming arms of the US Ski Team as a slalom specialist.

Meanwhile, the rest of the girls my age continued our progress along a much less spectacular path, plodding our way to each successive camp and hoping to get invited to the next one. It wasn't until nearly two years later that I was finally promised a spot on the ski team. I got injured the very next day. It happened that Nellie got injured in Europe on the same day, having barely missed qualifying for the 1984 Olympics, at only 17 years old. Instead of stepping into the spotlight she landed on our couch, next to me.

At first I was not thrilled for the company. In addition

to her on-snow talent, she was also physically striking—long and lean with well-defined muscles beneath smooth, tan Mediterranean skin. Spread out on the couch next to her, I felt the flesh on my belly and wished for the tight ripples of her stomach muscles. Outwardly, at least, she was everything I was not, and many things I wanted to be. I had every right to hate her.

But hating her close up proved impossible. My mother, a Bostonian by birth, delighted in having a fellow New Englander under her roof, someone who knew about boarding schools and frost heaves and fluffernutter sandwiches—things unknown to her own children.

"Peanut butter and marshmallows on a sandwich? Gross!" I was appalled. It sounded like something Elvis would have eaten in his later, slovenly days.

"I had them every day at camp," my Mom admitted, smiling guiltily. "For eight weeks."

"Mmmmm!" Nellie almost purred. "They're sooooo good." Then she turned to me, "And talk about gross. What about *orange* cheddar cheese? Real cheddar is supposed to be white. Orange is nasty!"

Mom was as happy to offer her wing as Nellie was to snuggle beneath it. I, too, developed a soft spot for Nellie once she disconnected from her constant undercurrent of intensity. Here on the couch, unthreatening to my own precarious ego, her sharp edges dissolved. She smiled and laughed and seemed to actually enjoy my company too. The next year, we again landed on the couch with twin injuries. Together we watched the TV as Donna, a shrimpy girl who wasn't even close enough to be in Nellie's shadow back at the academy, raced in Nellie's place at the World Championships. Now, three years later, we still resented everything about Donna's meteoric success, but we had each other as true friends.

I was ecstatic when Nellie showed up for a short stay that spring. I had just returned home from the last races of the season in Vermont, where we had headed straight from Vail, and she had flown in for a long weekend from Boulder to get her six-month check-up with Dr. Richmond. She hoped this check up would give her the go-ahead to start skiing in the summer. It was mid-April, the beginning of a three-week break that would be our longest until the following April, after the Olympics. Nellie was halfway through her spring term and already itching to be done with school.

I hadn't actually seen her since her last injury at our dryland testing camp in Utah last October. She had been whisked away quickly and flew straight to Reno, where my mother had met her and driven her to the hospital. By the time I got home from the glacier camp in Europe that had immediately followed, Nellie had already had surgery, headed home to Vermont and was preparing for her move to the University of Colorado.

This time I picked her up at the Reno airport and drove her back up to Squaw. Even though the mountains still hunkered under many feet of snow, the sun beat down hot in the valley, where the snowmelt off rooves and down culverts sounded like hundreds of wide-open faucets. Within moments of our arrival, Nellie had stripped to her tank top and settled into the exact spot on the couch where we had first bonded. It was right there, with our backs to the mountain, our injured legs stretched in opposite directions and a bag of Doritos between us, that we had watched the 1984 Olympics. Two dejected 17-year-olds, rivals from opposite sides of the country, shared the same common misery of watching friends and teammates rejoice in glory while we nursed our first blown-out knees.

"Blowing out" a knee is the common term for tearing your anterior cruciate ligament (ACL)—the main one that holds the thighbone (femur) to the shinbone (tibia) and keeps the knee together. For one thick band of tissue, it does its job darned well, to a point. That point often comes at 60+ mph, when landing unbalanced off a jump or when going from 60+ mph to 0 mph by way of a big orange safety net. That point can also come at very low speeds, as it did with Nellie her first time, when she fell back awkwardly while turning through a big wet pile of snow by the side of a training course.

However you sliced it, so to speak, blowing out a knee and recovering from the reconstructive surgery meant six months off snow, minimum, and at least another six months before you were full strength. Nellie's latest injury backed her right up against the clock if she hoped to recover her full strength in time to qualify for the Olympic team. The fact that this was already her third blown-out knee did not help the situation.

We had covered the basics on the car ride home. I knew Nellie had a new boyfriend in Boulder (no surprise), which roommates she liked and which ones she hated. There was no in between with Nellie. I looked forward to just the two of us really catching up, to filling her in on the latest gossip and hearing more about college life. I should have known we'd have company.

Considering how many people came in to Hotel California on an average day, the couch was also a plaza of sorts, a central gathering point where people met to exchange news for the day. Our front door opened into a long hallway. When visitors entered (sometimes after knocking, but mostly after not knocking), we heard them walk down the hall, and by the time they rounded the corner into view, all eyes were trained on them as if they were coming on stage. During Nellie's first visit, when everyone in the valley, it seemed, came to our house after the ski day to watch the 1984 Olympic broadcast, Nellie had learned how to distinguish the approach of all our regular visitors. We made a game of seeing who could guess the right name first.

We would sigh with dread when we heard the lumbering steps of Mick Taggart, better known as Mc Braggart, who sat for hours retelling stories of his role as an extra in the movie *Hot Dog*. Everyone in Squaw, it seemed, had a bit part in the movie—jumping off cliffs, battling for position in the "Chinese Downhill" or participating in the many après ski scenes. *Hot Dog* became the community's collective 15 minutes of fame, and being on crutches we had no way to escape hearing yet another account of the filming. Other footsteps had the opposite effect. When we heard the sturdy side-to-side gait—more suited to being places than getting places—and the crackling newsflashes of a German radio broadcast, we would both brighten and call out: "Hi Hans!" Around the corner came a stout man with a shock of tousled gray hair and twinkling blue eyes. He held a shortwave radio in one hand and greeted us with the other. "Servus girls!" he'd say in "Austrican," the hybridized language of Alpine dialects understood throughout ski country.

"Has the race started yet? This is going to be fan*tah*stic!" Before Hans found a seat on the couch, my mother would have engaged his empty hand with a full wine glass, making him race ready. On any winter afternoon, Hans might be joined by various coaches from Argentina, France, Switzerland and even Japan—all holdovers in one way or another from the 1960 Winter Olympics. The eclectic mix made Squaw, and often our living room, look like the United Nations of skiing.

In the off-season, however, visitor traffic seriously diminished, so Nellie and I were off our game when we heard the door open and shut decisively. The quick steps suggested no pretense of wanting permission to enter. We didn't have time to consult each other's gazes before Jamie rounded the corner to center stage.

After Nellie's first stay with us Jamie had been smitten. He called her all that winter and wrote her postcards from wherever he was racing; a minor miracle considering Jamie's distaste for all things pen and paper. He'd even written her a song that he played on his guitar and recorded. Even though they'd never been able to work out the long distance thing and both had moved on to other, more convenient people, she still traveled with the cassette.

"Hey!" This was Jamie's standard greeting whether you'd been gone for five minutes or five years.

"Hi Jamie. How's school?" Nellie matched his nonchalance. When it came to hedging emotions, they were both pros.

"Not bad. One more month and I'm halfway through."

"You still flying?"

"Yeah. It's still the closest thing to downhill. Sorta like my step-down program." He laughed a little, but I knew he was serious.

Jamie had basically been in a kind of re-hab ever since he'd quit racing, after his last knee injury in Argentina. It wasn't even a bad injury, but it was enough. The straw that broke the camel's back, as they say. But *he* didn't break. He might have tried to come back another five times, but the coaches told him flat out that it was over. Even though he knew they were right, knew he could not trick his mind into letting his body hurtle downhill at 80 mph anymore, he was livid. He'd been betrayed by the same coaches who had pushed him into World Cup downhills without enough experience, just because they needed more speed skiers. Once it became clear that their eagerness had backfired, that his talent had been used up in too many hasty comebacks, they wanted him to quietly go away. He expressed his anger by auctioning off all his uniform pieces right then in the lobby of the Argentinean hotel, to vacationers whose wallets were thick with $100 bills. He cashed in a tidy sum to ease his pain.

My Dad, in his usual pragmatic approach, made sure Jamie got right into college at the University of Nevada in Reno. Jamie was busy but with an aching void. Going from the thrill of World Cup downhill racing to the classroom in a matter of weeks had been a shock to his system. The only thing that had saved him was getting his pilot's license, which he did in record time. Now, in any free time, flying was all he could think about.

"I'm towing gliders in Truckee this weekend. Want to take a ride?" Nellie wasn't just being nice when she answered. Like Jamie, she couldn't resist a fix.

"I'd love to! Can we go over Lake Tahoe?"

"Yeah. We can go anywhere you want." He thought for a moment then added: "You're here for an appointment in South Shore, right?"

"Yeah. Tomorrow at 10. It'll probably last a few hours because I have to get checked out by the doctor and the

PTs. You know the drill."

"No problem. It's pretty slow at the glider port on Fridays. I'm sure they can cover me. On the way home I'll show you my best move. We circle behind the ski area, then go into a 'slip' and come over KT right there." He pointed to a notch in the mountain, right at the top of KT 22, Squaw's legendary ski lift. Jamie had shown me 'the slip,' a sideways strafing maneuver before, and I was sure most tech skier's wouldn't enjoy it. But Nellie would. Her eyes sparkled.

"Cool!"

That was about the last I saw of Nellie and Jamie all weekend. They did show up for dinner each of the three nights, and Nellie chatted easily with my mother while Jamie made more conversation than I'd heard from him in the past year. The two exchanged stories about college parties and cramming for midterms and the best apartments in Boulder. Jamie said he was considering transferring there which was news to all of us.

On Saturday night, Mom set another place at the table for Luke, my first boyfriend (if you consider someone you kissed on the chairlift when nobody was looking a boyfriend). He was up for the weekend from the University of California at Davis. Luke was older than me but we had been in the same grade in school. I figured out he liked me "that way" at a seventh grade dance, when we slow-danced to *Freebird,* all the way to the end of the song. His parents were university professors and had moved to Berkeley when we were in high school, leaving Luke to live alone at their condo in Squaw. When he wasn't throwing parties at his place he was at ours, dropping off laundry or having dinner.

"How is graduate school Lucas?" my mother asked, always using his full name like parents insist on doing.

"Not so bad. I started on some of the graduate courses last year, so it doesn't seem much different. I decided to just power through and get it done." If anyone was "too smart" to be a ski racer, it was Luke, not me. Not to be mean, but he had more wattage to spare than most of my teammates put together.

"And how is that dear Molly?" Leave it to Mom to always ask about the girlfriend. She just couldn't leave it alone and maybe let him forget about Molly.

"She's fine. She's working on a new line of clothes with a designer on campus. She's pretty excited about setting up a shop back home in Seattle someday. And, you know, she's keeping me properly dressed." Even my mom chuckled at this. Luke was the king of shaggy chic. He had a tall lanky frame that looked good in everything, but in his holey jeans and ratty flannel shirts he certainly was no slave to fashion.

Next she turned her attention to Nellie, asking first about her parents.

"They're good. Mom is, you know, working like crazy, and Dad is still in Florida." We never pried much about Nellie's parents. They had dropped out of college and lost their athletic scholarships to raise Nellie. They hung together for her sake but when she got picked up by the ski racing world their relationship finally sort of dissolved. Even though her mother was the one who always called to check up on her, it was her dad she idolized. He had never once called our house.

"Mom is dating some guy named Dennis. 'Dennis the Dork' I think is his full name."

My mom managed to stifle a grin and say, "Well, I

hope she's happy. Please do give them both my best."

After dinner Jamie and Nellie disappeared downstairs to watch MTV and discuss issues like whether David Lee Roth should have left Van Halen and if David Bowie really was gay.

My mom shooed me out of the kitchen which left Luke and me on the couch. Even though Luke and I had always been close friends, we had never been an official couple since our early days of chairlift ride dates. Sadly, pathetically, that had been the peak of my dating career so far. In high school he seemed to prefer non-skiing girls, pretty little Barbies who gave me a twinge of jealousy when I saw them nestled against his flannel-shirted shoulder as they drove past in his pickup. As we grew up, I had gotten used to being the girl who had lots of good boy friends but no real *boyfriends*. But that didn't mean I liked it.

Luke was more like a friend plus. We had traveled so much together—to local races and throughout the west and even once to Europe—that he was almost like a brother. He was so much like my brother that he, too, often stole my best friends and made them his girlfriends. But I had learned to live with that. Inside I quietly hoped that someday he'd "see the light" and discover my inner swan. We'd ski off into the sunset together as the credits rolled.

Then came the spring we received the same form letter from the US Ski Team, the infamous "hose letter" basically telling us to work hard and have a nice life. The US Ski Team didn't actually get to the point with those exact words but, when you held the hose letter in your hand, there was no doubt about its meaning. Luke was two years older than me when we got it, and that made a big difference. At eighteen and with no real faith in winning the lottery as a Plan C career path, he had to choose between college and ski racing. In other sports, Division 1 collegiate athletics are part of the path to greatness. In skiing, going to college full-time anywhere— even at a top skiing school—is seen as a career-ending decision. The hose letter apparently made the choice between Luke's dreams and his parents' practical view of reality clear. He would not, in any way, be playing the lottery.

Luke had scholarship offers from several of the top skiing schools, but he surprised everyone, even his family, by choosing U.C. Davis, which is dead flat, a touch below sea level and so hot that it never receives so much as a snowflake.

After he had gone to school, I kept beating down the US Ski Team's door, with constant encouragement from a father who practically begged me to "give it one more try," unlike most sane parents. My dad saw no reason why I shouldn't spend the years I'd earned by graduating from high school early on a wild gamble at making the US Ski Team. That said, he expected me to maximize any down time I might encounter. So it was, that a couple of years later, before the anesthesia had worn off from my second knee surgery, Dad wanted to know where I was going to "knock off some college credits" in my newly abundant free time. I chose Davis, knowing Luke had an extra room for the spring term. Of course I would also be living with his current girlfriend, the beautiful and self-assured Molly, but by then I was used to boy torture.

Instead of settling on the couch, Luke looked through the stack of VCR tapes next to the TV. He spotted *The Will Jackson Story*, a made-for-TV movie about the 1984

Olympic downhill gold medalist, the US Ski Team's most famous bad boy. It chronicled Jackson's life from his days as a minor criminal through his many battles with US Ski Team to his cockiness on the eve of the Olympic downhill, where he enraged the European downhill kings by predicting his own victory. Jackson had done time at the Hotel California, so he was our favorite underdog. When the movie first came out we had watched it together in Luke's apartment in Davis. Even though it was a fairly cheesy representation of ski racing, complete with too skinny, too pretty actors, we couldn't resist watching it again now. The race footage immediately pulled us in.

"Do you ever miss it?" I asked Luke, not really expecting more than a one-word answer. Luke's eyes stayed trained on the TV, and he spoke without a hint of emotion.

"Pretty much every day."

"So why didn't you go CU or Utah and race for them?" I knew Luke had been offered scholarships at both schools to race for their NCAA Division 1 teams. With all the Euros that Colorado and Utah recruited, he could have gone to school for free *and* kept racing at an elite level.

He didn't answer right away. I had already heard his standard reply, the one that relieved his parents and satisfied curious friends outside the ski world. That answer involved concentrating on school and making time for other interests. I knew that was a total crock. I thought maybe Luke was ashamed to admit that he wanted to chill out for a change and *just* go to school, which was enough for most kids. He kept looking at the TV, away from me.

"Do you know that I've put on 20 pounds of muscle since I quit?"

"Yeah!" Actually, I had noticed that he had quickly gone from boy to boy-man and was well on his way to man-man. But I quickly tried to cover my tracks. "I mean. Yeah, it makes sense. Most guys aren't even at their physical peak until they're in their mid twenties."

He turned from the TV to look straight at me, his expression still blank but his voice hardening.

"You know that and I know that. But the ski team doesn't know it. Or doesn't admit it. In four years, I'd have come out stronger and faster and the ski team still wouldn't have looked at me. I'd be in the same spot, just older. My parents wouldn't support me to just gamble away a few years waiting to prove myself. It's not like I'm a *girl*."

He didn't say it to be mean. It's easier for girls to make it in ski racing. We mature earlier physically and can be competitive internationally at a younger age. Plus an eighteen-year-old girl just out of high school pretty much knows her eventual size and has built her technique around that. She knows if she's "got it" or not. At that age, boys are still "a box of chocolates" in that you never know what's really inside. By the time they've revealed their physical potential inside, the US Ski Team has given up on them.

"What about the scholarships?" Didn't your parents want to take advantage of those?

Luke, normally so relaxed and upbeat, exhaled a terse laugh.

"They were so relieved I'd given up this 'nonsense' as they called it. They would have paid double tuition. After the whole 1984 Olympic team fiasco, Dad made a bet with me that all the guys they didn't take to the Olympics would quit. Good thing I didn't take the bet. He was right. There they were at 23, 24, 25—too old for a scholarship—with no education, no income and no career path. 'How's that for dedicating yourself to the US Ski Team?' my Dad said."

I stayed quiet.

"I love skiing and ski racing more than anything. I want to remember it as a good experience. *That's* why I had to give it up."

Just then he turned his attention back to the TV, and his face softened into a smile.

"Check it out—I think this is the part where he calls Franz Klammer a nose picker."

That was the last we spoke about racing, but I couldn't get the conversation out of my head. Luke was on track for a fascinating career, was happy and successful in school, had a great girlfriend—he had it all. But open him up a crack and he was suffering, hard, from what he didn't do. I had the chance he never got.

When it was time for Nellie to leave on Sunday night, Jamie gave her a ride to the airport. Just as well, I thought. Somebody ought to help Mom with the dishes and strip the sheets from the guest bed that may not have even been used.

I spent the next three weeks, my "off season," training at home and making the rounds on Interstate 80 to see my people. Driving west over the Sierras and into the Central Valley, I'd stop first in Sacramento to see my grandmother. She loved hearing about my travels, even the stuff I never dared tell my parents. "I never regretted doing anything I wasn't supposed to do," she once told me, with a mischievous glint. When I was at Davis after my second injury, I visited her often, sharing lunch by the pool in her lush, shady garden. Twice I brought Luke. The first time she raved about what a wonderful boy he was. "So smart. So handsome!" The second time he came with Molly. She never asked about him again, except once to ask if he was still with "that girl." I never admitted it, but I appreciated her allegiance.

From Sacramento I kept going west to the San Francisco Bay Area where both of my sisters lived. They worked in San Francisco, lived in separate tiny apartments and read the classifieds most every day, looking for a better, more exciting job. When I called them from the road, I tried not to complain about anything like the cold or the travel. Whenever I did, I was reminded that "it beat being stuck in an office making copies." They had a point. If college seemed daunting, being in the working world— the real world—was inconceivable.

But it was fun to pretend once in a while, to imagine putting on work clothes every morning like them, and getting on the BART train. I always visited over part of a weekend so that we could stroll around Berkeley or in the San Francisco Marina, sip lattes and talk about their various dates from hell. My best friend Marie was also in the city, working as an intern. I had envied her when I visited her at Chico State, the party school of all time. Her roommates—all of them boys—would laugh when they emerged from their rooms in the morning, still fuzzy from the night before and saw I was already back from a run and a trip to the gym.

"Marie's right," one of them said, emptying the unidentifiable liquid in a plastic cup from the night before and refilling the cup with water. "You ski racers are nuts.

Cool, but nuts."

Now when I visited Marie and heard her describe her daily routine of fetching coffee for a lecherous boss and collating reports, I wasn't so jealous.

These short brushes with reality reinforced that I was pretty committed to making my Plan A work. The plan had evolved and become more specific. It was no longer enough to become a famous ski racer. "Making it" meant winning an Olympic medal, perhaps getting on a Wheaties box and being set for life. Never mind that none of the medal winners I knew—and I knew a few well by now—had made it onto a Wheaties Box. I could be the first. I'd even settle for Pop Tarts. "They're good enough for me, so they're good enough for you," was the tagline Nellie had suggested when I told her my scheme one time over Doritos and misery. We had laughed then, but both of us assumed that if you did something that great, you'd be set for life. Being set for life seemed like a good thing to be.

Chapter 7:
Mt. Hood—This is only a test

Off season. When you get to a high enough level in any sport, even a sport that requires a frozen landscape, there is no such thing.

Everyone on the team was required to attend a dryland training and testing camp in Salt Lake City in May. Everyone, that is, except Lucy, who was at a "Battle of the Stars" celebrity athlete charity event in Hawaii, and Donna, who was just being Donna. She had some minor undetectable injury that required complete rest.

"Probably on a white sand beach," Anna had commented when we arrived at camp and discovered she had weaseled out of yet another dryland camp.

This was the first of three dryland training camps scheduled between now and the racing season. It was one more than usual because everything, it seemed, was ramped up. The urgency I had sensed amongst the Trustees in Crans Montana was now a full-on panic. The Olympics, once a distant ripple on the horizon, were now an incoming tsunami, and the order sent from up high was the same, only louder: Work harder!

After that first dryland camp, we reconvened on skiing's most popular volcano. Although most of us had been on snow in May for some sort of fundraising race and schmooze, or for informal equipment testing, our first official on-snow camp was in June on the Palmer Snowfield at Mt Hood, Oregon. From a distance, Mt Hood looks like a giant upturned ice cream cone, permanently frosted white with snow. Throughout the summer, the US Ski Team always seems to have a group here, but it is the commercial camps of eager Junior and Masters racers hoping to get an edge with year-round skiing that dominate the scene. This is where the business of ski racing happens. During the summer, Mt Hood's slopes and Government Camp, "Govy," the little town at the base of the mountain, literally crawl with young ski racers.

Govy is the buzzing hive of summertime ski racing, an industry in itself. The unofficial mayor of Govy was a guy named Todd, a rep whose small stature and general swarthiness made him appear gnome-like. Most reps are either technical reps, who select and maintain race equipment for top athletes, or sales reps, who sell their products to retailers. Todd was both. Over the years, he had taken on so many new product lines that when his van's back door opened, "stuff"—all manner of recreational toys—literally came rolling out. Because he was so short and had so many toys, we called him the Toddler. The Toddler's behavior typified that of an aggressive rep. He showered the high profile athletes with the latest new gear and attention, and lured the hottest young skiers to his products with stickers, keychains, t-shirts and an endless supply of cheap but cool trinkets. He reminded me of the childcatcher in Chitty Chitty Bang

Bang, except instead of stealing kids he signed them to long-term contracts.

"It's kinda like picking stocks," I overheard him explaining to a waitress at the local hangout, the Huckleberry Inn, as he sipped on a "world famous" huckleberry milkshake. "If you can find winners early in their development, you can get them real cheap."

The Toddler had an uncanny knack for his trade. He had sponsored me with poles and goggles when I was 13 and still winning every race I entered, when my coaches told the newspapers I'd be a World Champion someday and when I earnestly believed them. He had stuck by me for all of the next seven years, when it seemed I might never even make the US Ski Team, when Ken kept finding ways to block my path, when injuries kept me on crutches more than on snow. Now that I was one of "his" skiers, with as good a shot as anyone at the Olympics, he made sure everyone knew it.

"Hey Sharpie!" He called from his van. The kids all turned their heads towards me. "Try this on!" He tossed me a sweatshirt with a giant set of neon pink goggles silk-screened across the front. It seemed everything we were given to wear had some sort of neon accent, if it wasn't completely bright pink, the most popular color of the scheme. This latest offering was borderline hideous, but I'd wear it just like I wore everything else. You could pull off anything in a pack, and somehow it became cool. As I caught it and stuffed it in my backpack, the kids looked on enviously.

"Thanks" I yelled back, and already the Toddler was swarmed by the crowd of kids, looking to score some good swag.

It still seemed strange to be the object of even modest

hero worship. At the end of the ski day, the kids piled their gear around their team vans in the parking lot and waited for us to come off the mountain, building courage in numbers to ask us for autographs on their helmets, skis or parkas. I wondered if all those girls who dreamed of being in my boots someday, who figured I had "made it," had any clue about what "making it" meant. Or what it didn't mean. I was just starting to understand that "it"— whatever we thought we wanted to achieve—would never be enough. Once you got the uniform, you needed to make the World Cup team, and once you made that team you needed to make the Olympics. The more Olympians I knew, the more I understood how much they all wanted to win a medal, and if you won a silver you wished it were gold. A gold medal. Surely that would be enough. But Linda, the gold medalist I knew best, was struggling to regain her momentum, wondering why skiing fast, something that had once been so easy, so natural and so fun, now felt like walking uphill in sand. As for the medal, it hardly made a difference in her day-to-day life.

"Sometime's it's a 'Get out of Jail Free' card and sometimes it's a burden," she had once told me. I didn't understand what she meant until I saw her signing autographs and overheard interviews. The questions were always the same: "Are you going to win another gold medal?" or more bluntly from the reporters, "What's happened to your gold medal form?" and "What's happened to the US Ski Team?" If I had a bad day, nobody noticed. But once you win a gold medal, your bad days are everyone's business.

My first experience at Mt. Hood had been at the Shootout. Then, we stayed in isolation, 20 minutes further down the hill from Govy, in a town called Welches. From there we had packed into vans for the 30-minute drive past Govy and up the access road to Timberline Lodge. As the name suggests, the beautiful historic lodge is nestled into the mountain, where the trees give way to a massive expanse of white. From there, skiers board the Magic Mile chairlift by 7:00 am and ride it up Mt. Hood's gentle lower slopes to the base of the Palmer Snowfield.

It was on the Mile, riding down after a typical morning at the Shootout, that Anna and I first connected. The coaches didn't speak to 15-year-olds like the two of us, with no ski academy pedigree, except to assure us that this camp didn't really count for anything. "It's just for experience," they maintained, looking vaguely towards but never right at us.

"Yeah a bad experience," Anna observed as we rode down from the snowfield that afternoon. We had seen each other at the Junior Olympics that spring but here on the chairlift, discovering a new and shared insecurity, was our first real conversation.

"Have any of the coaches talked to you yet?" I had asked her.

"Nope. Not even two words."

I brightened. "Oh, I have you beat then! One of them did say two words to me. When he bumped me with a bag of salt he said 'scuse me.' That counts right?" They used 50-lb bags of salt to firm up the snow in the summertime heat. We both laughed. Not the kind of laugh that you do for joy (after all, what's fun about getting hit with a bag of salt?), but a little stress relieving one.

"It sort of feels like they don't want me here. I mean, we *are* the best they've got, right? So how come I feel like I'm not good enough?"

I knew how she felt. We glided quietly over barren

black volcanic sand with its hardy, scrubby bushes that gave way to twisted wind-gnarled trees. Their fight for survival in this wind-scoured moonscape reminded me of what I'd learned in school about Charles Darwin and his theory of natural selection. About how, even in the most inhospitable environments, organisms that are best suited to the conditions or adapt to them best can survive, while those that can't adapt, slowly die off. I looked at the plucky tufts of green and imagined how strong their roots must be. I imagined how every tough sprig of them had managed to grow despite constant abuse by Mother Nature.

"Darwinism" I said under my breath.

"Huh?" Anna followed my gaze to the bushes that grew hopefully, towards the promised warmth of the desert and away from the driving wind that howled in steadily from the Pacific.

"You know—survival of the fittest and all that. This camp is a form of Darwinism. They're trying to find out who can hang on longest." She looked at the inexplicable green emerging from the gray grit while I kept rambling. "But it's faster. Instead of having generations to adapt, we're supposed to figure out how to thrive in a week."

"Yeah, maybe." She sounded skeptical. "Or maybe they're big fat jerks." She definitely had a point.

Six years later, here we were. Of those 30 girls who had convened at the Shootout, the "future of the US Ski Team" seven remained. And of the Fabulous Four, who had eventually earned the coveted spots on the team that summer, only two remained. The rest had quit or been kicked off the team. The exercise of pitting young athletes against each other athletically and socially, while simultaneously ignoring half of them, had merit as a social experiment but not as an athletic training method.

After you get off the Mile, the Palmer lift tilts up more steeply to the top of the snowfield that hangs beneath Hood's looming cindercone summit. The skiing part of the snowfield stretches across an evenly pitched rectangle of smoothly groomed snow, bordered on all sides by refrozen sun cups rough with volcanic grit. The skiing area is divided into 12 or so equal swaths of salted snow—consistent top to bottom—that from a distance resemble inclined bowling lanes down which skiers hurl themselves lap after lap. Their even pitch and surface make the lanes ideal for the repetitious tasks of building fundamental skills and testing equipment. Both are an ongoing exercise for ski racers.

One of the main goals for this camp was testing, getting every bit of gear dialed in before our major summer camp in Argentina. Boots may be the most customized and critical piece of equipment—with all the factors like flex, footbeds, sole thickness and canting that have to be just right, to the millimeter—but picking a quiver of perfect skis for each event is the most labor-intensive part of gear testing. Ski testing was our top priority at Mt Hood and, as ever, getting it right depended on having a great rep. Sales reps make their living selling the products they represent (their line) to stores, but tech reps make their living by showing how well those products can perform. Unlike the Toddler, who was a sales rep most of the time and a tech rep when needed, full-time tech reps—at least one from each major ski, boot and binding company—traveled with the team year round. There was a Rossignol rep, a Dynastar rep, a K2 rep, etc. When an athlete got really good, she had her own rep. So, the Swiss had Maria's rep, Michaela's rep, etc. The reps picked skis directly from the factory then had their athletes test them to find the favorite and fastest skis. In Europe, reps are regarded with equal or more respect than coaches, because their job is so critical. Reps get paid a salary but make most of their money from "victory schedules" or bonuses that go along with their athletes' success. When Gus was fired, Sylvan—another Swiss and the rep for our top skiers—knew his fortunes would be better by following Gus and the Swiss racers than sticking with us under the Cheeseball's guidance.

Not surprisingly, after Sylvan's departure the performance of all "his" girls plummeted. He was still getting the best skis from the factory, but they weren't for the Americans, and the people hired to prepare our skis were far less experienced than Sylvan. Before last season, Natalie had finally switched to a smaller ski company that promised to build skis to her specifications. That might not have made a difference to most skiers, but Natalie had an uncanny ability to deconstruct a ski's performance and know exactly what was right and wrong with the ski. The company wanted some downhillers on their skis, so I had switched as well. For me, it wasn't much of a risk because, honestly, if the skis were good enough for Natalie, they'd be good enough for me. The few times I had skied on a pair of her skis, they had felt like Cinderella's glass slipper. Finding the glass slipper amongst a pile of look-alikes was an entirely new process to me.

Phillipe (Natalie's new rep and mine, too, as long as I stayed on the World Cup) had bags and bags of skis for us to test—easily 30 pairs—all of them labeled with numbers that indicated a wide variety of constructions and flexes. Some days we would be on a different pair of skis each run and, for consistency we tried to ski each run exactly the same way. At the top, I scribed tightly controlled arcs down the side of the frozen corduroy lane, then gradually opened up my turns, loosening my ankles to let gravity take over and let the skis seek their way into each turn. Turn to turn, I gained speed and built rhythm underfoot until I came to the moment of trust when one ski's energy rebounded me across the hill, momentarily weightless into the next turn, and I lay the ski over waiting a split second for its edge to bite into the snow that was just starting to soften under the mid morning sun. When it drifted into the turn easily, bit at just the right time, held for just long enough, then launched me into the next turn so that I landed balanced in the center of the ski, the rush of power simply told me I had a keeper.

Natalie, however, could give a detailed evaluation to Phillipe. I would see her occasionally giving him a thumbs up but more often shaking her head a bit and pointing to a section of the ski that didn't feel quite right. She didn't critique skis like Lucy (who, after seeing a bad training time, shoved the skis at her rep and said, "These suck!") or Donna (who said she liked everything then waited until the start of the season to decide that, actually, she didn't like her skis and would they please find her all new ones). Natalie's observations were much more thoughtful:

"The tip is too stiff. I can't get it into the turn."

"The tail is too stiff—it's bucking me around," or "The flex is uneven—there's a flat spot underneath the binding," or "These wash out in the turn—they're not strong enough torsionally." She could even tell what material was within the ski.

"These have a sweet wood core," or "What are these made of, Styrofoam? Ick!"

"Mon Dieu!" Phillipe said to me after Natalie took off

to test another pair of skis. He shook his head in amazement and smiled.

"Working with Natalie; it's like working with a thoroughbred. It takes a lot of work to get her into the gate, but then you just stand back and let her run."

He was right. It had taken a full year of Natalie working with Phillipe to get the skis just right, but things were turning around, and while Donna and Linda—the other stars the team depended on—were still searching for a way back to the top, Natalie—the vet at 25—was regaining her superstar form.

I could barely remember a time when I hadn't idolized Natalie. She was four years older than I was, and by the time she was fourteen she was already touring with the national team. By fifteen she was racing on the World Cup. On her ever-briefer trips home, she sported the latest in racing fashion: Vuarnet sunglasses from France; next year's skis; and always a dazzling US Ski Team uniform. Her long braid tucked down the back of her parka and peeked out the bottom. She walked straight as a ski pole, like the queen of skiing that she was. She was also nice to the little people and always asked how my racing was going. I liked her for that, and I also liked that she hated running and soccer. It gave me hope that even if I hated those things, maybe even *because* I hated those things, I had a chance at becoming a great ski racer.

Her house in Squaw was on my walking route home from the ski hill and, as a kid, every time I passed it I paused to look up at the windowsill that ran the length of the house and was lined with trophies and cups. As much as I idolized Natalie, a part of me blazed with my own possibility. After I had won a race, people would ask me, "Are you the next Natalie Scott?" I would smile and laugh shyly in a way that seemed to say, "Awww shucks I could never be that good," while inside I thought, "No, I'm the first Olivia Sharp."

Seeing how much I depended on Natalie, first for inspiration and now for guidance, gave me an inkling of how much we, as a team, needed her. In fact, we needed a lot more Natalies, not just to ski fast themselves but to show by example all the little and big things that we could take control of to help us ski faster. Ironically, I realized that ever since making the US Ski Team, thinking for myself had been discouraged.

It was better with Sepp and Dan in charge, but they were only two coaches. When most of the coaches and reps gathered at the bar at night, they laughed at the same old joke which, like all jokes, was rooted in a true belief. Life would be much easier, they fantasized, if the athletes would just shut up and ski. No complaints, no opinions, no wrenches in the plan. I'd have liked nothing more than to shut up and ski. However, I was learning from Natalie—when she made a stand on coaches or equipment or training methods—that if you don't speak up for yourself, nobody else will. I guessed that's what Dan had meant when he told me to "ask for my skis."

Off the hill, Ken, who constantly admonished us to guard our downtime and rest whenever possible to optimize our training sessions, asked for volunteers nearly every afternoon. The sponsors needed action footage of us for their Olympic commercials. We'd get paid well, but still it took hours to get one decent shot of a Subaru driving up and four athletes piling out, or a snowball fight that produced just the right Kodak moment or a smiling face chomping into a granola bar with the proper enthusiasm.

"It's just for an hour," Ken would promise. Even though we were staying right up at Timberline Lodge where they were filming the commercials, the volunteers would return partway through dinner, still in their ski clothes, exhausted and annoyed. Some ads, like Rolex and Chap Stick, needed the high profile athlete of their choosing (and buying), but most settled for anyone in a uniform. Fortunately there were plenty of rookies to fill the void, and there was Lucy who loved to jump in front of any camera.

Lucy, in a matter of months, had transformed into a "lean machine," as she described herself. Where there once had been grabbable rolls, she now had drum-tight abs, and any part of her that used to jiggle had disappeared. This sculpted version of Lucy was very different from the one in the mirror in Vail. She had worked hard starving and sometimes running twice a day to get swimsuit ready for her Hawaii event. (The Prozac helped, too, but that being "confidential," we weren't supposed to know about.) She was eager to show the new and improved Lucy to the world. She had found the "it" she wanted; an "it" that unfortunately had nothing to do with skiing.

Chapter 8:
Fighting Weight

"We need to work harder. Harder than we've been working and harder than the Europeans." Ken delivered some version of this inspirational message at the beginning of every camp that summer. It wasn't even his message, really, but the party line handed down from the ski team president who was trying to assure the Trustees and sponsors—all of whom had paid a small fortune to be associated with a team Ken assured them would win a trove of medals—that they were getting their money's worth with us.

Although the Cheeseball was only the messenger, he took full ownership of the mission: we would do more of everything—more on-snow training, more dryland training camps in Park City (oh joy!) and more training at home in between. Instead of lifting weights three times a week, we'd lift six times a week, alternating upper and lower body. Meanwhile, we'd increase our distances running and biking, and beef up our plyometric power workouts for good measure. Instead of one camp at Mt. Hood, we'd have two. Instead of two dryland camps, we'd have three, and test at each of them. All this looked virtuous on paper but, in practice, it left little time to recover in between. Already by our July dryland camp—the toughest one of the year, the one that even Donna couldn't manage to dodge—people were wearing thin.

Dan and Sepp took control at the on-snow camps, but at the dryland camps GI Jeff was back in charge. The trainer for the 1984 "Dream Team" retired with his gold medal resume to start a celebrity personal training business in L.A. In response to panic from above, Ken had re-enlisted him to "whip us in to shape."

"My job is to push you beyond your limits," Jeff assured us the first day of camp. "To break down each and every one of you physically and emotionally, then rebuild you stronger as a team." It sure sounded like fun.

"Dig deeper! Don't give up now—finish strong!" A lab tech stood next to the treadmill and, under Jeff's glare, yelled at Greta who was red-faced and panting. It was unusual to see Greta suffering physically, as she had been trained to perfection first by her parents and then by a hard core Hungarian coach at the academy. She usually cruised through most workouts. Here in the lab, though, everyone got pushed to her limit. For someone like me, who was routinely pushed to my physical max, like a draft horse in pursuit of a pack of gazelles, it wasn't unfamiliar territory. But for others this suffering and the berating that went along with it was a new experience. Not everyone reacted well to it. Despite being hooked up to both a respirator and heart rate monitor, when the lab tech yelled another round of "encouragement," Greta managed to reach out and punch her squarely in the chest without breaking stride.

One of the rookies got so freaked out by the barrage

of military-style barking and the unrelenting intensity that she shut herself in her hotel room, soothing herself with candy bars and tears until the coaches sent her home. I felt her pain, sort of. I still dreaded every dryland camp but, now that my spot on the World Cup team was secure, I didn't stress about my scores and focused only on improving them. By this time, I'd discovered a few of my actual strengths—quickness and rhythm, core strength and balance. Even though those skills didn't directly translate into many of the tests, they were some consolation. And of course I always had my mother's reminders that "our strength grows out of our weaknesses"; "Nobody is great at everything, and everyone is good at something;" and the ever-inspiring (especially from one's mother) "Sweetie, you have many wonderful talents." To give my mom credit, I had already witnessed the wisdom in her words and seen how working on weaknesses rather than letting them bum you out could be key to success, or at least to survival.

If my scores were less pathetic than the year before, I felt satisfied. Knuckle push-ups on the searing track? It'll pass and the blisters will heal. Hyperventilating at the top of the stadiums? That, too, was fine until Anna started laughing at me which got me laughing, which made me hyperventilate more and made Jeff send the whole team for an extra lap up and down each row of stairs. I may have gotten a pit in my stomach every day the van exited Interstate 80 and drove the final minutes to the University of Utah past bank signs that reported 100-plus degree temperatures. But all of it was doable. Almost all of it.

No matter how comfortable I became with the physical suffering and psychological indignities of dryland camp, one demon still terrorized me: the hydrostatic body composition test. My heart raced and my stomach turned every time I approached "the fat tank."

Inside a small room in the fluorescently lit lab, a plastic frame hung from a scale and rested just below the water surface in a raised tank. A lab technician gave directions from a platform beside the tank:

"Grab the front of the frame with both hands. Rest your knees on the back bar. Good. Now stay still." The tech recorded the number on the scale.

"Now, blow all the air out of your lungs and let yourself sink underwater. As you sink down, keep blowing and force all the air bubbles out. Then keep still so I can get a reading. I'll knock on the side of the tank when you can come up." I felt sick. I'd rather run stadiums until I puked than do this. But down I went.

Hydrostatic testing was no big deal for the lean, wiry "sinkers" who settled right down for a quick reading. But I was what they call a "floater" with body fat that typically hovered around 20 percent. For an average woman, that would be fine. The hard-bodies were nearer 15, and there were always a few workout psychos like Rebecca and now Lucy who were in the 10 percent zone. They'd pay for that in their childbearing years, I rationalized.

My relatively high percentage of body fat made me sink indecisively, which made the scale bounce around while the tech kept hoping for a better reading (surely she can't be *that* fat) and I, trapped underwater, began to panic. I shook uncontrollably, rendering the scale unreadable. When the tech finally knocked on the side, it was usually to tell me cheerfully: "Let's try that one more time."

What made the whole ordeal worse was knowing in my heart how little the test meant. In skiing leaner doesn't mean faster. If anything it usually worked the opposite way. I would never forget how, on my very first racing trip to Europe, Ken made fun of the "heifers" in the lodge, "chowing down" on salami and cheese while we nibbled on whatever we'd stolen from the breakfast table, usually apples and stale trail mix. The heifers smoked us every run. On that same trip, Gus had complained: "Ken tells me not to coach dis girl because he tinks she is too old or dat one because she is too fat. Too fat?! Cheezus! You girls should all *gain* ten pounds, fur 'die Kraft'...the *power*. Has he looked at the Europeans? Has he seen who is winning? *Cheezus*."

We didn't need to look far for negative correlations between performance and weight loss. Already, I'd watched some of our best skiers, in my era and in the previous ones, get obsessed with losing body fat and in the process totally lose their edge. Part of it was the purely physical effect of losing weight but part of it was about losing a vital part of themselves—their joy. I knew that dark place all too well.

As a kid I was always sturdy but strong; short but flexible and proportional. So, it wasn't like I woke up one day and suddenly discovered a body I hated. I'd been working up to it for a long time, with some outside help. When I was 12, I remember being quietly excited about being featured in a piece about hot young athletes for *New West* magazine. When my mom brought the issue home, I quickly flipped to the picture of me then scanned the article. I stopped when I read the words "chunky 12-year-old" and tears welled up in my eyes. I was crushed and, without reading any further, discreetly buried the magazine deep under the piles of other magazines and newspapers on the coffee table. I didn't care what the article said about my talent and bright prospects or about my coach's prediction of me being a World Champion. I only saw "chunky."

At the Jr. Olympics, when the boys and girls from different divisions convened, I held my own even amongst the guys on the hill. Off the hill, we laughed a lot together and played foosball and had snowball fights—but none of them liked me *that* way. When the Jr Olympics were over, none of them asked for *my* address and phone number.

At 14 and halfway through high school, I'd still only had one official date; if a double date with my sister to McDonalds and *The Exorcist* even qualifies. Every Friday when it seemed like all the girls wore their boyfriends football jerseys, I wondered why I wasn't boyfriend-worthy. I had always left my insecurities behind when I was on the ski hill, but suddenly little comments stuck in my head—the academy coach who credited my speed to "all that momentum she carries across the flats," and the thin pointy-nosed female coach who said I was really quick in slalom, "for a girl your size."

Just as I'd done with the magazine, I stuffed all the comments and feelings down. I let them simmer until one day in late summer, all that anxiety inside me must have quietly boiled over and I stopped eating.

I didn't cut back and try to lose a few pounds. I stopped eating altogether, and I found that starving was easy. That kind of control felt really good. By the time school started, I had lost ten pounds. By October I'd lost another ten and with it my entire sense of humor. For a while people said I looked better but, as the ski season approached and I dipped below 100 lbs, the praise disappeared. My father demanded that I add "real food" to my diet of alfalfa sprouts and coffee. My mother, who despite never having been overweight religiously tried every fad diet, seemed to cook up more of my favorite foods, suddenly presenting thick slices of cinnamon toast instead of letting me get my own breakfast. Her efforts only strengthened my willpower.

My sister, Laura, had gone through a similar transformation when she was my age, before any of us even knew the term anorexia nervosa. Now in college, she worried from afar. Whenever she called, I faked an upbeat voice and assured her that everything was fine. Mom and Dad were just overreacting. Meanwhile, Jamie thought he would help by getting my parents off my back. He assured them that my worsening mood was nothing more than a pre-existing personality flaw. As proof one day, he polled every one of his friends about my general demeanor. At the end of the day, he proudly announced the results of his informal survey: "See Dad, everyone agrees—she's always been a bitch!" That helped.

Mostly my friends moved further away from me, probably because they didn't know how to help. When my best friend Marie and her mother approached me about eating more, I figured they were both jealous and paid no attention. When our ski club's uniforms arrived, I picked the smallest one they had and proudly took it to our local seamstress to get it taken in. Paula the seamstress had dated the most gorgeous eligible bachelors in the Tahoe area and was the "it" girl I feared I'd never be. Just being in her fern-filled cabin, listening to Eric Clapton in the background and feeling the swingle vibe made me feel cool. When I stripped off my jackets and sweaters she didn't disguise her shock.

"Whoa! Isn't that just the tiniest little bod! What

happened to you?"

"I lost a little weight."

"How'd you do that?"

I thought back to what I remembered eating earlier that day, in fact every day that week. "Sprouts and coffee…and apples and tomatoes." (I had added Granny Smith apples and cherry tomatoes to my repertoire to placate my dad).

She dropped the subject, and we chatted about her latest fabulous trip to Mexico. When we were done and I was headed out the door, she took me by both shoulders and gently spun me so that I was looking right at her.

"Listen girl. I'm not really sure what's going on with you, and you don't have to tell me. But don't take this too far. As for the cute girls, trust me, you don't want to peak too soon. And as for the cute boys, they aren't all they're cracked up to be."

None of this counsel had any effect because—strangely, perversely—I started that season skiing faster than ever. The first race of the season, in Mt. Bachelor, Oregon, was also my first real downhill race. The downhill there features big jumps that are, not surprisingly for Oregon, often shrouded in fog. The combination of weather and terrain makes it a challenging downhill and a worthy test of guts and skill, two things every successful downhiller needs. I didn't know if I had what it took to be a good downhiller yet, but I knew the feeling I got at the bottom of each training run—the jittery feeling of being on the edge of something and of being scared but wanting to get closer.

The coaches interpreted my ability to throw myself down the hill at full speed in all conditions as a sign of fearless aggression, but part of my speed came from knowing that the quicker I got down the hill, the quicker I could get some clothes back on and get warm.

On the last day of the camp, Blake Gibson, a 17-year-old who had just been named to the US Ski Team, summoned me to his table in the cafeteria. I could barely speak from excitement that Blake Gibson, *the* Blake Gibson, even knew my name, and I hurried over. Before sitting down, I made sure to shove my parka underneath my butt to get some padding between it and the hard round plastic seat. He was eating French fries, and I had a pack of saltines. This was lunch.

"Have some fries," he offered.

"No thanks."

"Go ahead, have some," he suggested.

"No, I'm fine."

"Have…some…fries," he ordered. His piercingly blue eyes would not let me out of it. I had a fry.

"You know, you're really good."

"Thanks." I hoped with all my heart I didn't have any booger pieces stuck in my nose.

"But you're going to have to start eating. You have to be strong to run downhill. As good as you are, you can't keep it up unless you start eating."

I said nothing. He forged ahead then with his personal take on girls and weight.

"It's just weird that girls all feel like they have to be so thin. Can you really look good without being healthy?" he asked, not waiting for an answer.

"Look at the top downhillers on the World Cup. Are they thin? Look at even the top US skiers. Not the ones your age or a few years older who are trying to get boyfriends and kiss up to their coaches. Look at the ones who don't have to play by all that garbage anymore—the ones who are fast year after year. Are they skinny little things?"

I tried to envision the posters in the team room and the films we sometimes watched when the weather was too nasty to train. "Pixie-light Perrine Pelen of France" (the subject of one of our favorite play-by-plays) was tiny but, if I really worked on recalling the images, I saw mostly strong legs, thick torsos and solid arms that could knock a gate out of the way at 50 mph and not bruise.

"Do you want to be thin or do you want to be fast?"

I had to think about that one. Being strong had always been a good thing in our house. Even when I was eight years old and Dad summoned me for piggyback rides around the dining room table and then had me tighten up my stomach muscles to resist one of his punches; it was a show of his pride and mine. Nobody in my family had ever made me feel bad about being strong or looking strong. But what if I could be all those good things and be thin too? That would be perfect. That would make me happy. So, here I was thin and fast. But I wasn't happy. I wasn't even *un*happy. I didn't have energy to spare on any kind of emotion. The only thing that had given me any kind of emotional jolt lately, that had made me care, was downhill racing.

I thought about my conversation with Blake for most of the eight-hour drive home amidst the constant arguments about what cassette to play (Queen, Pat Benetar, Led Zeppelin? The Donna Summer tape had been banned within an hour on the way up.) I didn't know guys even thought about this stuff, and here the object of my hero worship—a guy I barely knew—had cut right through to the truth my friends and family never dared to touch. Tricky.

Blake made the choice seem so simple. Thin or fast? I so wanted to be both. Some people *could* be both, but not me I suspected. Not if being thin sucked all the joy out of life as it had done for me. That night I got home late after everyone was asleep. My goal, when I had left, was to lose another pound before coming home, so I got on the scale. 94 pounds. Mission accomplished. Then I sneaked into the kitchen and looked in the freezer for something I hadn't had in months. Ice cream. I scooped out a bowl of peppermint ice cream, sat down and savored it slowly in small spoonfuls. Thin or fast?

I chose fast.

Just because I'd made that choice all those years ago didn't mean I was entirely happy about it, especially at times like this, crawling out of the fat tank. Even though I knew that being a floater was my natural state, I sometimes wished for just a touch of anorexia, a way to turn it up and down as necessary like a thermostat. If only I had that power, then whenever I overheard Jeff refer to me as "roly poly," my physique might not seem like the life sentence that I suspected it was.

On the last day of camp, Ken handed each of us a thick report analyzing our results, compared on bar graphs to the rest of the team and our own prior results. In the past, I would have squirreled mine away in my duffel bag before anyone could see it, even though the results went to anyone who asked for them be it a coach, sponsor or trustee. But this time I thought I'd done a bit better, so I was looking the report over in the hotel lobby.

It was the usual: in the vertical jump, the 40 yd dash, the 440, I was solidly at the bottom. In body fat, I was right at the top. But in between were a few promising results: not bad on the 12-minute run; good on flexibility, sit-ups, push-ups; near the top in the hellish bench jumps, a test of quickness, rhythm and sheer will. If we found ourselves in a dance contest, I'd be in business. Anna was looking over my shoulder. I had forgiven her for laughing at me in the stadium and by this time we had no secrets, so I didn't mind her looking at my results.

"You're like the Kentucky Fried Chicken of ski racing," she said, shaking her head and smiling.

"Excuse me?"

"You know, you do one thing and you do it right."

Strangely that quasi insult made me feel better. If I couldn't be good at all things, at least I was good at the things that mattered. It still made me mad—the body fat itself and the fact that I was always apologizing for it—but at least now I was starting to feel like I could put it on its proper shelf, always present but out of my way. If GI Jeff wanted to rave about lean and mean Lucy, to hold her up as the successful "after" shot to my "before," I could live with it.

One thing dryland camp was always good for was making me look forward to our camp in Argentina. Just get me on snow, I thought. Let me tap into my inner KFC, let me do the one thing I am supposed to do, and do it right. Then we'll see who's lagging.

Chapter 8:
South for the Winter

You're all clear!" Sean nodded to me, and I planted my poles over the starting wand. Dan and Sepp had radioed up to him that the middle and bottom sections of the course were all clear for my run. Straight out from the ridge where I stood, a craggy black hunk of the Andes reached into deep blue space. For as far as I looked in all directions, there was nothing but rock and snow and sky. Way down below, a tiny cluster of red-roofed condos and hotel buildings that looked like 3-dimensional triangles wedged into the snow marked the valley floor.

August is the middle of winter in Argentina, and the remote resort of Las Lenas had just gotten pounded by a monster Pacific snowstorm. Then, just like at home in the Sierras, the sun had come out and turned the treeless rocky moonscape into a brilliant winter paradise. There's nothing to do *but* ski in Las Lenas which is why I loved it. From where I stood at the top of our downhill course, there were just dots of red-paneled downhill gates, acres of snow and 3,000 vertical feet of high speed skiing between me and the bottom.

I pushed out of the start, and the fluttery mix of adrenaline and nerves quieted as I dove into three big turns on the steep upper pitch. Once up to speed, I laid my skis over into a sweeping right turn, pushing my legs into the snow to resist the G forces that pulled me down towards the ground. I drove my hips, knees and ankles into the hill to counteract the centrifugal force pulling me outside the turn. As I approached the first big jump, I straightened my skis down the fall line, pulled up my heels and rolled my shoulders forward. One big jump launched me into silence, until gravity returned me softly back to the track that seemed to magically come up from below. Then I shot down the pitch into the sweeping turns on the lower section. My skis hummed louder as they gave friction the slip, accelerating over terrain that rolled beneath them in a perfect rhythm. Tip into the turn, dive over the rolls and press down on the back side, milking every nuance of terrain for speed.

One good run of downhill, feeling that initial anxiety overtaken by sensations of power and freedom, would convert anyone to the sport. In Las Lenas, we often had six or eight of those runs a day. Downhill here bore no resemblance to December's opening World Cups where the lack of both snow and daylight conspired to create icy, dark, bumpy courses from hell, and where everything seemed to have a hard, cold edge. Here I could ignore that reality and be completely smitten by downhill at its best.

On my way back up the first of two chairlifts, Dan gave me two thumbs up. From the next lift, I looked down to Sepp who merely nodded which, from him, was a high compliment. Most of the time his comments, if he made them at all, included the suffix, "Goddammit" as in,

"Rebecca Goddammit, let your skis run!" "Sharpie Goddammit look ahead!" Some days it felt like Goddammit was my last name. But like a true Austrian, Sepp was passionate about skiing, understanding it as a skill and as an art. And, unlike Ken, he fully appreciated and endorsed the free-spirited aspect of serious athletes. As long as we did our job on snow, he didn't try to control the rest of our time. Also unlike Ken, Sepp used few words and was brutally honest. He was the proverbial Russian judge, incapable of giving false praise and the first one to tell you when you sucked.

We came all the way to Argentina to get miles—lots of miles on winter snow. After a morning of training on nearly deserted slopes we headed in to lunch, just as the resort guests were emerging from their condos to settle into the lounge chairs that lined the sunny, snow-beach outside their condos. They smiled over their café con leche and toast, and waved at us sleepily from behind dark sunglasses. Most of the guests didn't even go out for dinner until 10 pm which explained why the slopes were empty all morning. Our sit-down lunch, served on china with perfectly pressed white napkins, usually featured "Lomo" (steak) so outrageously delectable that it had converted more than a few vegetarians. We didn't get many vegetables except for the shredded lettuce that looked like what they fed the local llamas so, if you didn't eat one of the three major road food groups (meat, pasta or French fries) you didn't eat much. After lunch we headed back up the mountain.

Some afternoons were reserved for downhill ski testing. Unlike the giant slalom ski testing we did at Mt Hood where we tried the skis in multiple turn shapes and in as many different situations as possible, downhill ski testing was, literally, straightforward. The reps set up timers at intervals along a straight track, then hauled huge bags of skis by snowcat to the track. These weren't "our" skis per se. They were the companies' skis. Whoever was skiing fastest at any given time got the fastest skis.

We stripped down to our race suits (which have been described as shoulder length panty hose and are just about as warm) and tucked down the track run after run, each time on a different pair of skis, getting towed back up the track by snowmobiles. After 20 or even 30 runs, we were almost in a meditative state from the repetition. I say "almost" because it's hard to meditate when you're freezing your butt off.

Sepp was a big believer that cutting loose on a big steep mountain is better than any official downhill training so, on the afternoons when we didn't have to test skis, he set us free to explore. Most everything in Las Lenas is named after planets or constellations which is fitting for a place so rugged and remote that it feels like another planet. Our favorite place to make laps after training was on the Marte, or Mars, chairlift. Marte rises 2,500 vertical feet (two Empire state buildings) nearly straight up the side of a craggy mountain. From the top, we could drop into chutes and bowls that plunged into the valley below. One day Anna decided to spend her free afternoon racking up runs on Marte.

"I'll bet I can ski 50,000 vertical feet in an afternoon," she predicted.

"That's 20 runs," I pointed out in case her math had gone downhill as fast as the rest of her routinely went. It would be like skiing from the summit of Everest to base camp…five times.

I just want to see if I can do it." Anna was like that—

always looking for something to push her limits. One time, after she hung up from yet another unsatisfying phone conversation with her mother about the "club championships," I asked about her decision to give up the tennis scholarships. "Don't you ever wonder how good you could have been? Like if you could have gone pro?"...and made a lot of money is what I was really thinking. Without hesitation she answered my question with one of her own. "Where would you rather be? Chasing a yellow ball and staying in the lines or letting it all hang out, screaming down the side of a mountain?"

Anything Anna did, she did with 100 percent of her energy. It was absurd that Ken used to tell her she didn't work hard enough. She could bench press a pair of "manhole covers," the big 45 lb weights, without breaking a sweat and could squat twice that. The only thing she couldn't do well was run long distances, a skill virtually unnecessary for Alpine skiers. But that and her healthy weight was enough to justify Ken's criticism.

It all changed the year she won the Nationals. She had won a giant 30-lb Toblerone for her efforts and when Ken suggested she give it to the course workers to "save herself" from it, she bent down, encircled the giant triangular bar in her arms and stood up to face him.

"Save *yourself* from it!" She stepped forward and swung the bar like a giant baseball bat, cracking it across his butt.

From then on Ken shut up about her weight.

I rode with her for the first run of her 50,000 vertical foot quest but, at the top I turned right to explore some chutes. "Have at it. I'll check in later."

Towards the end of the day, I joined her for the final push. Even sitting on the chair, her quad muscles twitched involuntarily. We both looked down at them. "Now *those* are some sewing machine legs," she said proudly.

We were used to reaching this state of exhaustion at our dryland training camps but not usually while skiing. Ken had wanted to dissuade Anna from her mission, tell her not to waste her energy on this skiing marathon. But Sepp had stopped him with his trademark simplicity.

"You can't be great at anything unless you love it. Don't mess with the love."

Marte was already deep in shadows and was about to close when Anna finished her 20th run with an exhausted, satisfied smile on her face and collapsed at the bottom of the lift.

"And the prize is...all-you-can-eat lomo!" I joked, pulling her up by her ski pole.

Sepp was the first to congratulate Anna on her feat, toasting her with a glass of ever-present Fanta at dinner. If her legs were a little sore for a few days, if she needed to back off on her dryland training, no matter.

His bigger concern was Lucy. As our top downhiller going in to an Olympic year, Lucy was in high demand by all the press back in the States, and she was thrilled to oblige them with interviews and appearances. Her bikini diet, the antidepressants she had started taking (according to "confidential" information leaked by a team psychiatrist), and her intense aerobic conditioning had combined to turn her into a chiseled specimen. Throughout the summer, she had hustled to get her picture in every ski team sponsor ad which only made her more body conscious.

At first I was jealous of her Jogbra-clad image, but any six-pack-abs envy disappeared when we got on skis in

Argentina. One afternoon I was watching video with Sepp when Lucy appeared on the screen.

"Who's that kid on the course?" I asked as a tiny body flopped around the top turns. I recognized Lucy's arm and hip position, but nothing else about the passive skiing looked like her. A bump knocked her off course. The old Lucy would have cranked on the ski and brought it back around in an instant, but I watched as she teetered through the rough snow outside the course and struggled just to stay upright. It looked like her legs might just snap off.

"Crazy diet!" Sepp grabbed the remote and, after that, fast-forwarded through every one of her runs. "Lucy, Goddammit! She's not going to win any medals eating twigs and sawdust."

Lucy ate "only this" and "none of that," and we all wondered when she would start ordering "only the plate." Beating Lucy in time trials was no longer a challenge. She barely had enough strength to get through a session of ski testing because she got so cold. I tried to talk to Lucy about what was clearly a problem. Many years later, I still remembered the complex feelings of anorexia clearly; the unrelenting struggle to stay in control. They say you never really get over it. Every time I tried to bring up eating though, she offered me diet tips, like suggesting I eat raisins if I really wanted a sugar fix. She probably thought I was jealous. I remembered that, too. Sepp was already shifting his top hopes from Lucy to Linda, our only speed skier with Olympic experience. Linda had weathered a few rough years sorting out coaches and equipment, but she was rediscovering her form. That ability to win didn't just go away after all. But it liked to play hide and seek.

One afternoon at the bottom of the course after a

training session, Jenna, a girl who had been fished out of college to boost the ranks of our downhill team at the end of last season, picked a wrestling match with Linda. A collegiate athlete getting picked to join the US Ski Team was a surprise anytime, but especially in an Olympic year. Considering the randomness of it all, Jenna couldn't help but have a lighthearted approach. She was a lot like Lucy in her younger days—strong, loud, obnoxious and funny when she wasn't mad at you. She was sort of like a rambunctious puppy always looking for the next playmate. Linda was the perfect target. She didn't love running, biking or lifting weights but if you offered up a game she would play until she dropped.

"C'mon you gold medal wussie. Show me what you've got!"

Linda's eyes lit up. "Bring it on, rookie!"

The two went at it, lunging at each other then rolling around on the snow. We were all laughing until we heard a pop, and Linda cried out, clutching her knee. Our ace in the hole, our Olympic champion, flew home the next day. We later learned the prognosis: she would likely recover in time for the season, but she would lose the entire preparation period. This was a definite bummer and not at all good for Ken's master plan.

Usually when stuck in one place and packed six to a condo, we would have been at each other's throats going into the third week. But one key factor kept that from happening; the men's team. Being in the same place with them had two huge advantages: first, watching them ski, with their added strength and power, brought up the level of our skiing; second, some of us—ok, maybe most of us but particularly Lucy and Anna—behaved a lot better when the men were around.

Those two had never been close. It went all the way back to the Shootout, when we had endured Lucy belting out Broadway show tunes on every van ride to and from Timberline. (She had confided that she had to choose between being a child star and a ski racer.) "Where is her kill switch?" Anna had quietly pleaded on one of those torturous journeys.

Lucy wasn't from a ski academy—she was from a small ski area in the midwest with a strangely big reputation for creating top ski racers. But at the Shootout she had instantly assessed the competition for valuable allies, and attached herself to the academy girls. The one time Anna had tried to join Lucy on a walk to the store, Lucy had accelerated, linked arms with one of her new academy friends and broken into the chorus of "Just the two of us!" without looking back. Since then, it had seemed like Lucy went out of her way to dis Anna.

Finally, while in Argentina the previous year, their shared and intense interest in boys and socializing had brought them together. Once they bonded, it was as if Lucy's pure lust for skiing infected Anna and brought her skiing to a higher level. They pulled the rest of us in their wake. Lucy's confidence rubbed off on Anna in other ways too. For the first time since I'd met Anna, she quit apologizing for her weight. It was that confidence, finally, that set her free of Ken's criticism and allowed her to wield the giant Toblerone.

"Who's coming to the disco with us?" Lucy, called out to our condo-dwellers. She waited by the door, her hair straightened, teased and sprayed into an impressive raven mane. She wore the brand new expensive black leather jacket she'd bought on our shopping day in Buenos Aires. It was practically a requirement to buy a leather jacket in

BA on our layover, but this time Lucy had bought two—one black and one white—along with the tight red leather pants she now wore. Lucy was leading the charge for an evening out. The prospect of a party was enough to conjure up the old Lucy we knew and, at times like this, loved. A huge storm was blowing in and it had already snowed over a foot, so we knew we wouldn't be skiing the next day. Storms like this usually lasted at least three days. Because the disco didn't even open until eleven, it was a rare chance to visit the boys in their rooms and then go dancing and blow off some steam. They were scheduled to leave the next day, but we all expected the storm would change that.

Rebecca looked up from her book: "Didn't you hear what Ken told us? He said nobody was supposed to be out past 10, even before a day off."

Rebecca must have been the kid who reminded the teacher about homework right before the bell rang at the end of the day. Maybe that's why the Cheeseball had liked her so much. More likely, he just liked looking at her in her racing suit.

Lucy rolled her eyes. "Let me guess. Anyone he catches is on the next plane home."

I remembered the ice cream incident on my very first, very miserable Europa Cup trip, in which Ken said he was going to send us all home for "borrowing" a barrel of ice cream from the hotel's freezer. Even with the trouble we got in, it was the most fun of the entire trip. All of us with some experiences on the wrong side of Ken smiled at his favorite threat.

"He also said nobody is allowed to sell any part of her uniform," I said, looking at Anna, who was concentrating on the important task of applying eyeliner. Anna always packed the most luggage, and this time her giant duffel bags had been crammed with every piece of US Ski Team clothing she had ever owned. She had already made a tidy sum from wealthy Argentines who paid an obscene amount of money for anything bearing a US Ski Team patch.

"*Real* champions probably don't stay out late or sell their uniforms." I teased.

"*Real* champions don't have any fun," Anna countered.

I always welcomed the opportunity to go out. We didn't even bother asking Greta, the original real champion and the clueless butt of our joke, who was burrowed into her bed reading a book, with a teddy bear tucked under her arm.

Our first stop was one of the boy's condos. Lucy and Anna both had boyfriends at home, but that didn't stop them from flirting relentlessly. I didn't know it but tonight they had decided to help my prospects along. Everyone knew I had a crush on Blake Gibson. The boy who had seemed completely beyond reach when I'd first met him, when he was a 17-year-old US Ski Team member and I was a 14-year-old nobody, was now in my zone. He and Jamie had become good friends on the downhill team, so I'd gotten to know him well. He'd even stayed at Hotel California during the "Storm of '82" when it snowed over 15 feet in ten days, and everyone who had come to race the National Championships in Squaw was trapped wherever they happened to be staying. In the midst of the storm, I'd celebrated my 16th birthday with four of the cutest "older boys" on the US downhill team. Three years no longer seemed like such a big age difference when it was 21 to 24, and the fact that we were both on the Word

Cup team further evened the match. My longstanding crush on Blake was no secret even to him, and increasingly he seemed to humor it. I always knew where he was on the hill and tried to be in position to ride the lift with him whenever possible. Lately he seemed happy to oblige me.

When we showed up to watch *Caddyshack*, our favorite of all the movies we knew by heart, he made room for me on the couch and offered me half his blanket. My happiness could not have been more obvious, even without the blushing.

From their room, we made our way to the disco, which was just as smoky as the European discos but bigger, less crowded and somehow less hopeless feeling. They played straight pop music—tame stuff like George Michael, Whitney Houston and Billy Ocean—not the synthesized techno re-mixes that the Euros loved. It felt like a place people came to celebrate life rather than escape it. The vacationers made it seem almost like a cruise ship, and we came here with a pure quest for joy.

To my surprise, Blake kept wanting to dance with me. Every once in a while I bumped into Anna on the dance floor, and she gave me the thumbs up. It felt like the other guys were watching us, too, and when the Romantics' "*What I Like About You*" played, I was sure he was singing right to me. I wondered if the entire men's team knew about my crush too. Not that I cared. This night was too good to question.

When Lucy and Anna told me they were leaving, I saw that it was already well after midnight. *La Bamba* was blaring so loudly that I pointed at my watch and stood on my tiptoes to get near Blake's ear.

"I have to go."

He nodded his head and walked over to a cluster of guys who were resting between dances. I saw him say something to them, then reach for his coat.

"I'll come with you." At this point, I was pretty sure this was a joke or a dream. I didn't care which—I just didn't want it to end. He took my hand and led me along the side of the dance floor towards the door for a discreet escape. Before we could get there, one of the guys yelled:

"Hey Blake! Where are you going?"

Everyone turned to look at us. He pulled me on to the dance floor, spun me around, dipped my head back over his arm and planted a long kiss on my lips.

We ran out the door to a large round of applause and a chorus of cheers in Spanish. Just outside the disco, we stopped, breathless and laughing, and he kissed me again and put his arm around me. That's when we noticed Anna and Lucy clapping.

"Finally you guys!" Anna said smiling. She tipped her head back to look at the sky as if sharing the news with the heavens. Immediately her smile disappeared, and she sucked in her breath as if she'd seen something really scary. We all looked up and were hit by the same realization.

"Stars!" We'd have to be on the lift by 8:30. I looked at Blake and lifted my hands in a helpless gesture.

"You've gotta go. Thanks—that was fun tonight." He gave me a long hug, winked (his way of saying "I'll call you," I decided), then headed towards his building. Lucy, Anna and I raced back towards our condos, hoping the coaches wouldn't see or hear us.

We hadn't technically broken any rules by going out because Sepp and Dan were pretty loose, especially knowing the beneficial effect socializing usually had on

Lucy and Anna. Although we didn't know our exact limit, 1 a.m. was definitely substantially over it. So, we tried to be quiet when we returned to our building with our clothes reeking of the cigarette smoke that had filled the disco. The bow in Anna's hair was drenched with sweat.

"Do you think we can put this in our training log?" Anna whispered.

"Three hours of dancing or walking all the way down the hall on our toes?" Lucy whispered back.

I was suppressing a giggle right outside the coaches' door when it suddenly opened. Out came Sepp, dressed and ready to go out. Behind him his room was brightly lit, hazy with cigarette smoke and filled with the sounds of Latin-American music and international laughter. He met our look of surprise with a smile and quickly put his finger to his lips.

"Guten nacht!" He winked at us and softly shut his door behind him.

The next morning when we loaded the lifts, too few snow cats were busily attempting to groom too many training hills. Miraculously, our downhill was the first to be totally buffed out. When the snow cat was done, it stopped and the driver called to Sepp while giving him a friendly wave.

"Hola, Amigo!" The cat driver was just close enough for us to see he was wearing a brand new US Ski Team vest with the coach's patch still on it. Sepp knew how to get things done.

On our last day in Las Lenas, we had GS time trials on the Marte lift. Anna and I were looping around on the chairlift together, both feeling giddy on this crisp sunny day. It seemed we couldn't help getting faster each run; by the fourth run, we were beating most of the technical skiers. Both of us fantasized about someday competing on the World Cup in all events, so any day that we could stack up to the technical skiers was a good day.

"I love this place!" Anna tilted her head all the way back to take in the sky. A pale fingernail moon hung just above the rocky ridge that ringed the horizon. I looked up, too, taking a deep, satisfied breath. This, I thought, is paradise.

"Uh oh—there's a cloud." The wind up high was spinning thin clouds out of nowhere and then dissolving them. Anna took her ski pole and aimed it like a gun at the cloud. Instantly the cloud disappeared. We looked at each other amazed, then spent the rest of the ride "shooting" the clouds away. At the top of the lift, we lowered our "guns" and put our hands through the wrist straps. Still looking up, Anna smiled and spoke into the sky.

"I feel like we can do anything!"

Chapter 9:
Flying High

Traveling back and forth from Argentina, from summer to winter and back again, is like being in a time warp. We'd go from the height of summer—days filled with mountain biking, trips to the lake and outdoor barbecues every night—to traipsing through the Miami airport (where we all convened for the flight to Buenos Aires) with ski boots slung over our shoulders. Once down in Argentina, we quickly and happily slipped into mid-winter mode. But still, the hot humid blast of reentry in Miami was a comfort. There's still time to get ready, the thick summer air promised, still time to build up strength to get through a long winter.

That's part of why I loved September. And I really loved this September. Everything, it seemed, was coming together—the skiing, the coaching, the potential boyfriend. I wasn't naïve enough to think the third part of the equation was a done deal. One night of dancing and a few kisses didn't mean much in a traveling ski racer's world, especially a ski racer like Blake. Just like in the movie *Downhill Racer* (the best ski movie ever), the men's circuit has a tribe of groupies; star-struck girls in every resort, who throw themselves at anyone on the World Cup start list. They threw themselves particularly often at the downhillers and particularly hard at Blake. Still, I thought he'd made some sort of acknowledgement about me, about us, that boded well. "The future's so bright, I've gotta wear shades." Every time I heard that song— and it seemed to be on everyone's mixed tapes that summer—I smiled as if it were written just for me.

Another great thing about September is that it is gorgeous everywhere, especially in the mountains. The tourists are gone, the air is a touch crisper and the weather is still perfect for hiking, biking and communing with the mountains that are both sanctuary and competition arena. Some days I'd hike to the top of the Palisades at Squaw, or bike the flume trail straight above Lake Tahoe's turquoise water, or jog up the Pacific Crest trail and skip lightly over the loose rocks and boulders on my way back down the trail. "Deer bounding" one of my coaches called it, and there was no better way to develop real agility and quickness. It felt like the mountains themselves were feeding me, making me strong, putting their arms around me one last time before sending me on my way for this big season. In anticipation of the intensity around the corner, I looked forward to wringing every golden, peaceful moment out of September.

Ken had other ideas. He had booked many of us, coaches included, for the "Turkey Tour." One of our sponsors was a lunch meat company, and they had requested that athletes show up at their sales meetings and corporate headquarters to inspire employees. Some of the trips involved riding in the company's private jet, "Air Turkey" as Sean called it. Others were decidedly less glamorous guided tours of bologna factories. The trips only took up a couple of days each, but they involved yet more cross-country travel which intruded on this last stretch of rest, training and downtime. The top stars like Natalie and Linda, were excused from the "Turkey Tour." Ken hadn't even dared approach them. Donna got out of it with a sinus infection, a recurring ailment she used conveniently, and Lucy got out of it by claiming vegetarianism.

The rest of us not only had to talk turkey but also had to show up at the various ski balls; black tie fundraisers at major cities throughout the country. It was sort of fun for one night to get a free makeover at Macy's, put on a fancy dress and pretend to be both female and grown-up. Lucy did show up for those high profile events even though beef and chicken were usually on the menu. I had hoped that Blake might be at the San Francisco ball I attended, but they sent us to the events closest to our respective homes, so he went to Denver. I took Jamie as my date.

By now Jamie was finishing his undergrad degree at a college in the San Francisco Bay Area, though he flew home to Squaw most every weekend. As much as my father envisioned him in a business suit, it wasn't in Jamie's make-up. Two things were in his make-up: downhill racing, and flying. Now that one was over, he immersed himself in the other. After getting his pilot's license, he was adding every advanced rating he could so that someday he might again make his living in the air. He managed to find a tux for the ball, and apparently he looked pretty good to the parade of beautiful single women he danced with—women who knew how to do their own make-up and had more than one dressy outfit I assumed. But Jamie hadn't protested when it was time to go. "They all look like plastic," he had complained. Compared to Nellie, of course, though he didn't admit that.

The next morning was a typically gorgeous fall day in the Bay Area. "Want to do a little aerial reconnaissance?"

"Game on!" I never said no to flying with Jamie. We went to the Oakland Airport where he kept the single-engine plane he shared with a friend.

I didn't talk much to Jamie about skiing anymore, because his wounds from it were still so fresh. But this time he brought it up first. He wanted to know what I was working on with the coaches, how the other girls were doing. I told him about Lucy's weight loss and the way she kept blowing out of courses. He started humming Tom Petty's "*Refugee*," the song he used to sing to try to lighten me up during my hungry phase. When he sang it to me then, though, he had changed the words to: "Don't...have...to *look* like a refugee..." This time, I laughed.

Jamie always had a way of cutting right to the issue. I had grown up with coaches who employed every accent and teaching style: the French who dropped h's where they belonged, added them where they didn't belong and rarely said more than "or-ee-bull, terr-ee-bull;" the Argentines who made up for their rapid-fire, incomprehensible verbal instructions with eloquently delivered demonstrations, communicated entirely with their hands; the blessed Austrians who usually suggested "noch einmal," one more run, as a way to solve any problem. But the coach who influenced me the most was Jamie. I could count on him to tell it like it was, even when it wasn't pretty. He was my biggest fan and my biggest critic.

One time I blew out near the bottom of a training course because my legs were about to collapse in shoulder-high ruts. Everybody who had gone before me—even the much older kids—had blown out of the course higher up, and the French coach actually praised me for surviving as long as I had. "Pas problem Ho-leev-ee-uh. Eet ees honly training." But Jamie had watched my run and raced to the chairlift to catch me before I got on it.

"What the hell was that?" he demanded. "I don't *ever* want to see you give up. If you're going down, go down *swinging!*"

And that was his enduring advice to me, not matter what the circumstance.

We flew up the Sacramento River Delta, and he pointed down to Rio Vista, his favorite windsurfing spot. I could just make out the colorful sails, zipping back and forth across the gray muddy water. When he was still skiing, Jamie spent every moment of downtime searching for wind and waves. The sport takes spare time and money, two things he had a bit of while ski racing. The ski team, just like it did for me now, had paid all his training and travel expenses. The money he made from sponsors could fund necessities like cars, gas, food and windsurfing during his short breaks at home. Now school and flying took care of any excesses of time or money. I knew he was jealous of the life I still led, coming home long enough to do laundry then leaving on the next adventure before any part of life got to be routine.

We turned back towards home but he detoured south, high over the black smudges that were oak trees clustered on the flanks of Mt Diablo.

"You ready for some spins?" I didn't even look over at Jamie. I couldn't get up the nerve to answer because on one hand spins scared the pants off me. But I also loved the thrill of feeling the airplane quietly tilt up and lose speed. Just when everything became still, the stall horn would erupt in the silence. As the plane slipped backwards, Jamie would tip the wing sharply to one side to make the plane fall sideways then roll into a nosedive and fluidly pull out of it once air pressure returned beneath the wings. That sensation of recovery was so powerful, so triumphant, that it cleaned out every bit of tension hiding in the nooks and corridors of my body and mind. Imagining that feeling, I smiled which Jamie took as a yes.

We did spin after spin after spin. Nothing but silence and sky filling the windshield, then the rush of earth and forces and the roar of the engine returning to life. It became a kind of loopy rhythm and, just like a downhill run, each spin made me want more. Here in the air, I didn't have time to lose my nerve between spins like I did between downhill runs. It made me wonder. What if my fear wasn't actually a weakness? What if it was just a sign that I needed to do more of what scared me? That must be what the coaches meant by "getting miles" and building experience. I didn't know for sure because we never talked about it, but I suspected some girls never dealt with fear like I did, never went through the mental gymnastics I did just to get myself into the starting gate.

It's not that I was too smart to be a downhiller (as Ken brilliantly suggested), it was that my mind had a tendency to get in the way of my skiing. I wished I was more like Jamie and even Lucy, who thrived on that

danger and speed, who needed it to live. I liked it enough
once I was there and liked the feeling of getting through
it, but I didn't have the raw danger-seeking gene. Did I
really just need experience, or was I in the wrong line of
work?

On our way home, Jamie asked about Nellie. Jamie
hadn't spoken about Nellie since the one time he went out
to visit her in Boulder. I figured he had discovered the
other boyfriend and that had ended things. I hadn't dared
bring her up.

"She's coming to the camp in Europe to see if she can
qualify in time trials. If she's in the top five, she'll come to
Copper."

"Hmmm." Jamie cocked his head, assessing. "A
month too soon. That's about right."

"What do you mean? That'll be almost a year."

"*Almost* doesn't count in nuclear war and knee
surgeries."

"I don't think she has a choice."

"Probably not. Ken's such a weenie. I'm sure he made
a big deal about this being her last chance. But even if she
did have the choice to take her time, she wouldn't be able
to stop herself. It's her streakness."

Streakness? What the hell was a streakness? Still
monitoring the horizon through the windshield, Jamie
smiled slightly as if he enjoyed watching me try to puzzle
it out.

"Everybody has a streakness, a strength that's also a
weakness, part gift and part curse."

"You mean like an Achilles heel?"

"Not really. It's that thing that can get you to the top,
but only if you know how to control it. Lucy has her need
for attention. Nellie has to be tougher than everyone else.

These things motivate them but lead them to the same place every time. The press pumps up Lucy and by the time they've lost interest she's lost focus. Nellie comes back in record time but then gets reinjured. Either way it's a dead end. Hopefully they recognize the pattern and figure out how to change enough to actually move ahead. But some people just can't help themselves. Some people get stuck on the same script."

I wanted to hear more from Dr. Jamie. Clearly he'd taken Psych 101 and had spent some time applying it to his own experience.

"So how does Nellie's movie go from here?"

"Well, some of that depends on how she deals with the other actors, mainly Ken who controls her. He's got a classic Napoleonic Complex, little man's syndrome. He can't stand women, especially strong women. As long as he can keep her down, keep tempting her before she's ready, she'll keep getting injured and he won't have to deal with her. And if she does manage to stay healthy, he'll have been the one who gave her the chance. Either way he wins."

As much as I disliked Ken, I couldn't believe he was that sinister, and I told Jamie so. "That sounds a little like a conspiracy theory."

"C'mon O, you of all people should recognize it. Can't you see how his mind games almost worked with you? Luckily, *your* streakness helped you last time." I opened my mouth to ask, but Jamie was already barreling ahead in answer. "You don't really believe you belong, so you'll do anything to prove that you do. When Dr. Richmond made you quit downhill for an entire year, he didn't just save you from Ken; he saved you from yourself. Ken would have gladly let you throw yourself down a mountain at top speed even after two serious injuries in one year. And you would have done it. Hello injury #3. Luckily you didn't get the chance. Instead you had to find another way to prove yourself—in slalom. It was harder but it was safer. And you were just hard-headed enough to do it. Ken never saw that coming."

Jamie was right. I'd never forget sitting in Dr. Richmond's office when he gave me the news that might have ended my career along with a short course in ACL mechanics. Using a knee joint model to demonstrate, he had grabbed the top section—the femur—in his right hand and the lower section—the tibia and fibula—in his left hand. He bent the model knee so that the joint opened exposing a thick rubber cord—the ACL—that threaded from the back of the femur to the front of the tibia.

"This is how your knee is supposed to work." He moved his hands down towards each other and back up and apart, opening and closing the joint, as one might test the doneness of an enormous chicken leg. "And this is what happens in a downhill crash," he continued, "when you combine the forces of high speeds, a hard landing and long skis that act like giant levers." He pulled forward hard on the tibia with his left hand, while pulling down and back with the femur in his right hand, spreading the joint until the thick rubber ACL popped spritely off the top front of the tibia. Both of my knees started to ache. I might never eat chicken legs again.

In addition to banning me from downhill races indefinitely, he clearly described what types of exercises I should not do until my knee was fully recovered, if ever. I knew Nellie had seen the same graphic explanation and been given the same warnings because we talked about them the first time we were served roasted chicken at the Hotel California. And yet she never backed down from any exercises at the dryland camps, even the ones that were clearly dangerous. When she blew out her knee again at our fall dryland camp last year, it was while doing something quite obviously ACL-unfriendly, something we were clearly told to avoid.

"Nellie can't save herself," Jamie continued. "Her streakness is all about being tough, and every time she gets hurt she tries to come back faster than the time before. The coaches all remember how good she was and how good she could still be. Everyone around her wants her to take that chance; wants to believe that Nellie and her incredible slalom skiing can save the team."

I remembered what Gus had said about Nellie right after my second injury, when he was still my coach. We were trapped in a snowy Italian valley for days without power or phone. On the third morning of being marooned in our hotel he had scooped me into his Subaru and tossed my duffel bags and my homemade-by-the-handyman crutches in the back. Without a word he hit the gas, fishtailed past the road closure signs and gunned it over the pass towards the Zurich Airport. Once my knuckles released their grip on the door handle, I relaxed and spent the next four hours immersed in ski racing philosophy; Gus talked and I listened.

"The Americans want everyone to be winning World Cups by the time they are 18. Sometimes you get those att-letes like Natalie who can win at 17, 18. But most times you need to be patient. It takes time. Come back smart," he had advised. "Not so fast. Eat, train and rest. You push too hard and the injuries come. Look at Nellie. She is a 'special,' like Natalie, one of the greats that comes down from himmel (he pointed through the Subaru's roof). But she comes back full gas too soon. Trust me. One more year on the Europa Cup for confidence, and then you do it just like this on the World Cup."

Gus had been right. Even if it took doctors orders and one of Ken's backfired plans, I hadn't been reinjured. Nellie, on the other hand, had suffered several minor injuries and a third major one, again on the cusp of an amazingly fast recovery.

Back in the plane, we were flying steady now, heading back to Oakland. Jamie's face tightened when he talked about Nellie.

"If anyone cared about her, they'd stop her," Jamie continued. "But she makes it clear she doesn't want anyone to care about her."

Chapter 10:
High Pressure System

"Jesus!"

"Yes?"

"No, not you." Nellie was not amused as she plunked her bag down in the lobby of the Hotel Dom in Saas Fee, Switzerland. It was almost 8 pm, and Nellie and Greta had just arrived, half a day after the rest of the team.

"Please tell me the kitchen is still open."

"It is. And they promised to make any rosti you want." Rostis are Swiss country fare and a specialty at the Dom. They consist of meat and/or veggies (if you must) cooked to your choosing then heaped on a bed of fried potatoes and topped with an oozing layer of melted cheese. They definitely fall in the "heart attack on a plate" food group, but they are seriously tasty.

I wanted to ask Nellie about her trip but, by the don't-even-think-of-messing-with-me look on her face, I figured it could wait until after she'd eaten.

Saas Fee is a tiny mountain town one valley over from Zermatt, another tiny mountain town that has the good fortune of being smack under the distinctively shaped

Matterhorn. Except for the Matterhorn and the extra tourists it attracts, the towns are nearly identical. Both are ringed by awesomely huge peaks that are snowcapped year round, both prohibit gas-powered vehicles and are reachable only by train then electric carts, and both feature glaciers where racers flock during the summer and fall to train.

Every October we went to one of several glaciers, depending on what coach was in charge. For years, under a mainly Austrian coaching staff, we went to Soelden and Hintertux in Austria. Lately, however, an influx of Swiss coaches had led the women to Saas Fee and the men to Zermatt, just next door. Getting to Zermatt and Saas Fee is a trek even when all goes perfectly. From Zurich we headed south, then drove the vans onto a train through the Kandersteg tunnel. From there we drove through Visp and up the Saas Valley, then zig-zagged on an ever narrower road up the steep slope to Saas Fee. From the parking lot, we loaded our hulking 6-pair ski bags on electric carts belonging to the hotel and shlepped the rest of our stuff by foot to the Dom in the center of town.

That was getting there the easy way. Nellie and Greta had missed their flight in Boston and had to be re-routed to Frankfurt then Munich, where they caught four different trains and a bus to get to Saas Fee. If it hadn't been for Nellie, Greta wouldn't have made it past the ticket counter in Boston let alone all the way to this remote Alpine valley.

"They were going to charge us overweight for our ski bags, and Greta was just about to hand over all the money she had." Nellie recounted her journey over a bubbling-hot Rosti.

"And let me guess. There was no 'double star' in the

file?" I asked jokingly. The ski team's travel agent always promised that there was a special waiver in our airline records, a 'double star' that was supposed to tell the airline agent not to charge us for overweight baggage. If there was such a thing, none of us had ever had it no matter how many computer keys the airline agent punched. Plan B at the ticket counter involved our US Ski Team ID cards and a supply of pins and stickers that we used as bargaining chips. The only thing more ridiculous than the US Ski Team's assumption that these would help us was the fact that they usually did. Over the past few years, I'd probably checked thousands of pounds of overweight baggage for free, gotten bumped to first class and finagled free taxi rides all with a smile and a handful of US Ski Team pins.

"Shockingly, no double star," Nellie confirmed. "But I checked our skis outside and gave the skycap ten bucks." Another excellent tactic. Nellie had then figured out the next best airport to fly into, gotten them on an available flight, bought the train tickets in Munich—with the money Greta hadn't given to the airlines—and made all the right series of transfers to reach Saas Fee. "Greta couldn't even get a train ticket." Nellie, so self-sufficient out of necessity, seemed more amazed than annoyed.

We went to bed early in Saas Fee because the days started early. For the uninitiated, getting *to* a Swiss glacier in the fall is an athletic event unto itself. The trek begins with a walk with all your ski gear through the cobblestone streets of town, in brisk fall air that is as crisp as a fresh-picked apple. It feels like walking through a postcard in the morning quiet as you pass bakeries and shops and a few houses, their tidy front yards brimming with frost-kissed cabbages, kale and hardy cold weather crops. The narrow roads converge where the land rises up through a pasture. Right about then, electric taxis start whizzing by and the road becomes clogged with kids, coaches and equipment reps hauling huge backpacks of gear. By the time you reach the base station of the first tram or gondola—the first of several that will whisk you up some 7,000 plus vertical feet—you are part of a legitimate mob.

There is no such thing as civilized turn-taking in a European lift line. Tradition dictates one must earn the right to ride a lift by elbowing and pushing one's way forward; no small task amidst a sea of national team, junior national team and regional racers from throughout Europe. By the time you make it to the summit—by way of the Klein Matterhorn tram in Zermatt or the Metro Alpin train in Saas Fee—-you are rewarded with a view from what seems like the top of the world. The quaint peace you may have felt at the beginning of the journey is replaced by sheer awe at your surroundings.

Our first morning there was postcard perfect—sunny and spectacular. From the plateau where I stood, sunlight bounced in blinding sparkles off an endless expanse of snow and ice. Beyond the plateau, the glacier dropped sharply to the right and into a massive bowl unobstructed by trees and faintly dotted by a few T-bars towers.

"Sharpie. Try these." The Toddler suddenly appeared beside me. He was holding out a bright pink pair of goggles with bright purple lenses. I put them on my helmet, pulled them down over my eyes and looked out over the Alps.

"Wow! These are crazy! Everything looks so…alive." I couldn't think of another word for it. Inanimate objects—the craggy rocks, the letters on my skis, even the tiny ridges frozen into the snow—seemed to come alive and jump out at me as if the only thing keeping the world from crawling right inside my head was this one thin lens.

"It's called the 'Psycho lens'," Todd explained. "It was developed for NASA, and possibly a few of your teammates," he added under his breath. Then back in his regular voice: "It's totally high def, even in a snowstorm. So, do you like it?"

"Yeah. I think so. I mean, if I can handle it."

"Yeah, well apparently it's a little intense for some of the athletes. A few of them, well it sort of makes them sick to their stomachs. But the ones who like it, love it," he quickly added. "And I know you hate flat light, so I snagged you a stack of them."

"OK. Thanks. I'll keep you posted on the hurling part."

Lenses, helmets, boot buckles. By this stage in the season, we were all about fine tuning. All the major testing was done. On the way to Europe, all of us speed skiers had gone to Buffalo, NY, for a day, to the wind tunnel. It is essentially a tube with a giant fan at one end that creates wind speeds of up to 100 mph. The wind tunnel is mainly used by the automotive industry for car design, but it works just as well on humans that travel as fast as cars. One at a time, we clicked into a pair of skis firmly attached to the floor. A technician closed the door behind us and turned on the fan. A digital readout showed how much drag we created in various skiing positions so that we could tweak our aerodynamics and find the ideal tuck. When Will Jackson won his downhill gold in 1984 on attitude and aerodynamics, he gave a lot of credit to his work in the wind tunnel. Ever since then, it had become an integral part of our training. In addition to honing our aerodynamics, it was also the ideal venue for testing the official US Ski Team hair mousse as discovered by Jenna.

The Toddler came to the wind tunnel with us because he was also a ski pole rep and was somewhat of a savant at pole bending. For each of us using his brand, he custom fit two sets of poles that wrapped around our bodies perfectly when we dropped into our tucks. It was one more thing to try to get just right, one more way to shave a few hundredths of a second.

Every bit of prime steep space on the glacier was filled with a training course, and two downhill courses sprawled across the further side of the glacier from the top of the highest T-bar to the bottom of the lowest. This tightly packed busy scene—which looks and sounds like a vibrant international marketplace—is a timeless snapshot of ski racing's essence: fast, focused and intense. With an Olympics on the horizon, the atmosphere felt especially charged.

The glacier in Saas Fee tops out at over 11,000 feet. At that elevation, there is less oxygen to breathe, so our bodies have to work much harder to perform normal functions, let alone the things ski racers routinely ask their bodies to do at 60 mph. Because of that, plus the extra effort it takes just to get to the glacier—not to mention the jet lag—our energy ran down quickly. Normally coaches back off on dryland activity at these camps, to let the body recover after each training session on the glacier. When we came here in the summer, we spent most afternoons doing whatever activity we wanted. Anna would challenge the reps on the tennis courts, the academy kids would play pick-up soccer on the many turf fields and others of us hiked to the various huts perched high above each side of the valley. Even after hiking for an hour up a steep trail, we would typically arrive at a hut to find a couple of elderly women with walking sticks, totally unfazed by the effort, resting on a bench...smoking. The Alps breed toughness.

All these activities were purely summertime diversions. In the fall, ski racers should be focusing on quality, not quantity. Everybody knew that. Everybody, it seemed, but GI Jeff. He had come along to make sure we kept up with our regular dryland training in addition to the glacier training. What made matters worse was the high-pressure system that had settled over the Alps. Usually we could count on a few bad weather days for rest, but blue skies and perfect weather maximized our time on snow. Not surprisingly, little injuries started popping up.

A few days into the camp, we were playing volleyball and I came down from a jump and rolled my ankle. I actually heard it pop, and it hurt like something inside had seriously torn. Immediately Sean took me to his room, iced it and wrapped it and gave me some of his massive Ibuprofens shaped like mini submarines. I could tell he was worried, but he kept his mood light and assured me that ankles could heal remarkably quickly.

After just one day off skis, the ankle still looked horrible—all black and purple—but the pain had subsided significantly. I planned to jump right back into training. Dan came by my room and invited me out for a coffee that afternoon. He would do that occasionally and quiz me on what books I was reading, or discuss pieces in the literary journals he made me read. I guess I had a crush on Dan, but I never admitted it even to myself. He probably knew it too but he never let on. Clearly, however, he knew that a crush, when properly played, can be a powerful motivator. Around Dan I tried a little harder, complained a little less and read much longer books than I ever would have on my own.

He sounded more tense than usual, preoccupied with something more than literature. After ordering two velvety cappuccinos, we sat at a table by the window, and he got right to the point.

"We can't afford to lose any more of our top skiers. We have to keep you healthy, and it's not going to be easy." For God's sake, I thought to myself, it's only a twisted ankle. As if reading that thought, he continued: "I'm not just talking about this injury. If you start skiing fast in the technical events, and I suspect you will, there's going to be a push to put you in every time trial. And you will be so flattered, you will say yes. Am I right?" He did know me well by this time, or perhaps my streakness (along with my body fat percentage) was a matter of public record.

"And you want me to say no?"

"I want you to be smart. Someone is going to get hurt here. In fact we'll be lucky if it's only one. Don't be that person. Honestly, this injury is the best thing that could have happened to you. Take a page out of Donna's book, and use it to your advantage. Ski when you can, but just for a few really good runs, then use the ankle as an excuse to rest in the afternoons."

"What will Sepp think?" I still felt the need to prove my toughness to Sepp.

"Sepp wishes you'd *all* roll your ankles and get out of this ridiculous training schedule. He knows this overtraining thing is all a big show for the sponsors. But he can't say it. He also knows Ken is looking for a way to get rid of him."

"If you both know it's wrong, why can't you do

something about it."

"We're here talking aren't we? Look, it's beyond us. It's beyond Ken. It's not even about keeping our jobs. I know I'll get fired eventually. But we have to make it through the season together if we have any chance at all in Calgary and beyond."

"What do you mean about Ken and Sepp...and about you getting fired?"

"All the coaches who stick up for the athletes do. Nobody wants to stick to a boring long-term plan or do what's best for an individual. They all want a quick fix; the next great thing, a pretty picture and a catchy slogan. Right now. The guys that rise to the top are, well…"

"Like Ken?" I suggested. Dan almost managed to hide a grimace.

"Have you ever heard of the Peter Principle?" Here we go again, I thought—Dan turning a simple observation into a teachable moment. As usual, I played along. (Crushes do wonders for your social graces.)

"I think I heard my brother talk about it from one of his business classes."

"Yeah, that makes sense. The Peter Principle is a theory that was introduced sort of as a joke but it's a truth about organizations. It basically says that people get promoted to their level of incompetence. And then they stay there, incapable of moving up and usually unwilling to move down.

"But what does that have to do with Ken? He already suc—uh, was incompetent, as a Europa Cup coach."

"According to the Peter Principle, the real work is accomplished by employees who have not yet reached their level of incompetence."

"So, guys like Gus when he was basically doing his job

and Ken's?"

"And Klaus after him," Dan added. Klaus was an Austrian coach who came in after Gus had been fired. It only took one van ride to convince me that Klaus was certifiably nuts—full on, pass-on-corners-while-adjusting-the-radio, swear-at-other-drivers nuts. When he got angry, a vein on his forehead pulsated just the way it did with my third-grade teacher right before she started chasing kids with her yardstick. It made me nervous. But Klaus, though psycho in many ways, had the knowledge and experience we so needed. Like Gus he tried to convince Ken that we needed to race less and allow more time for training and recovery. Like Gus his advice was ignored.

"More shots on goal!" Ken would say, when explaining why we were trekking to another obscure village to get our butts kicked. Ken loved slogans like his favorite, "Win at every level!"

"How about winning at any level," Klaus would mutter through clenched teeth in response, the vein beginning to pulsate. Klaus only lasted a year.

"Ken even got promoted a few levels beyond his incompetence because he took credit for everything Gus and Klaus did. So he's even more dangerous. There's no way he can move further up the ladder, and he has a long way to fall if anyone knocks him off. His only prayer at keeping his job is to tell everyone above him whatever they want to hear and to get rid of anyone underneath him who makes too much noise."

"Well, that's depressing. And I thought it was just the Napoleon Complex that made him such a tool."

"Even more troubling is another part of the Peter Principle that says: Anything that works will be used in progressively more challenging applications until it fails."

"Which in English means...?"

Once again, while trying to follow one of Dan's conversations I found myself losing my grip on the tow rope. He tried to reel me back.

"Humans in general—not just US Ski Team coaches—are tempted to use what has worked before, whether or not it's right for a new situation."

"That explains GI Jeff and his hard-ass training techniques?"

"You got it!"

"So we're, like, an experiment."

"Well, yes, but to be fair that's not the way they see it. They—Ken and Jeff and everyone above them—think they are doing the surest thing by recreating 1984, but they're missing the point. I was there. I saw what went on. The '84 team wasn't any more talented or hard-working than you, but all of them—coaches, athletes and reps— had more experience. They knew that working hard and working smart are two different things, they knew how to get what they needed, they knew the importance of having fun along the way and they sure as hell wouldn't have dragged their asses around the country hawking turkey parts. Just this once, be more like Donna. It's not 'wimping out.' It's looking out for Number 1."

After two days off snow, I put my well-taped foot in a ski boot, and it felt surprisingly good. That's one side benefit of doing your sport with hard plastic casts on your feet. As advised, I used my injury to get out of the soccer and circuits and hill sprints that Jeff dragged everyone else through each afternoon. And as Dan predicted, two of the younger girls went home early on crutches and another broke her wrist. That many injuries in one camp was a disaster, but nobody dared make the connection between overtraining and injuries. As a team, we were still invested in winning the toughness award.

I spent some of my spare time in the ski room in the hotel basement, visiting my new rep Steve. In preparation for the Olympics, my ski company had hired a rep specifically for the downhillers, all two of us. Steve had never traveled on the European racing circuit, which probably explained why he was so mellow. Whenever I delivered him beer or chocolate I found him in a good mood. After the GS time trials, I was hanging out with Steve while he worked on one of the eight pairs of skis he had to sharpen, wax, scrape and brush for the next day. He handed me a paper with the times from that day. I had tried not to look at them before and to only focus on my skiing. But curiosity got the better of me. I looked at the paper. Natalie and Donna had won most runs, but I was close behind and amongst the top five tech skiers. Steve smiled as he saw me studying the results.

"What are you trying to do—leave me and be a tech skier?"

"Maybe."

"Man, we're going to need to bring a lot more skis to Calgary."

I was trying not to think about the Olympics. But we all felt the clock ticking, even here on the glacier, six weeks before our first race and four months before the Games themselves. In ski racing, there are no "Olympic trials" though many people, in rescripting their past greatness, claim to have broken a leg "just before the trials." The team is chosen from results in the season leading into the Games. The Olympic team selection criteria hadn't changed since 1984. You needed one top five, two top 10s or three top 15s in a World Cup to qualify. For someone who had never been in the top 15, I wasn't exactly a shoe-in.

It was Nellie's turn to shine in the slalom time trials. Even on the harsh glacier ice, which I knew was hurting her knee and making it swell up like a grapefruit every night, she made it look easy. I watched in awe from the T-Bar as Nellie made one of her runs This was the old Nellie, the real Nellie; relaxed, confident and flowing like liquid effortlessly down the hill. In four runs of slalom, she finished every one clean and was never out of the top 3. Now, finally, Ken would have to be on her side, even though he claimed he always was.

The men's downhill team came over from Zermatt to visit on our rookie night, an annual ritual to initiate the rookies by making them perform skits. The men's downhill team had originated the rookie night tradition. Their definition of a rookie was clear. Anyone who had not run the Hahnenkamm in Kitzbuhel, Austria, the hairiest downhill on the circuit, was a rookie. Each year at their rookie night, the vets awarded the "Rookie Rock" to the teammate most likely to make his Hahnenkamm debut, thereby graduating from rookiehood.

Convincing the boys to come over was easy enough, especially considering how much they loved rostis. The coaches didn't mind so much because it put us all in a better mood, and there was a built-in curfew. The last train to Zermatt from the parking lot in Tasch (the closest driveable town, seven kilometers below Zermatt) left at midnight, so the boys had to be back in Tasch by then.

I saw Eric first, as he walked into the lobby. As usual he was smiling and gave me a big bear hug. "Sharpie! I hear you're rippin' it up!"

"It's going pretty well. How are things on your side?"

"Great. The downhill is pretty gnarly. I had a few epic beaters but, other than that, it's all good. Still haven't gone home in a body bag."

The body bag reference came from something a Canadian racer had once said in reference to our downhill team's inexperience. "The Yanks'll throw anyone whose willing down a World Cup downhill. They ought to measure your boys for body bags, not uniforms."

The men joked about the comment, but the danger was real. A few men had died in downhill crashes, and many others had come close. Eric was like a puppy dog, and downhill to him—even with the danger—was just another way to play. Keeping him *away* from a downhill course seemed almost inhumane.

"Look what I got." From his backpack Eric pulled out something big and heavy with bright red, white and blue words crudely painted on it. The famed Rookie Rock.

"Do you have to carry it around all year?" I asked, touching the relic lightly with what I hoped was the proper reverence.

"Nah. It rolls around in the back of the cargo van until I can hand it off to someone else. But I wanted to show you guys, I mean girls." He truly beamed with pride.

Right behind Eric came Blake. I hadn't heard from him since Argentina. I so wanted to play it cool with him, to pretend I didn't expect any form of communication, but immediately I felt the blood rushing to my face. He looked at me sheepishly, not the way you look at someone you're excited to see, and then gave me a short hug. I had nothing to say and nothing to lose, so I opted for humor, the easy out.

"Did it hurt much?"

He looked at me, sheepishness replaced by confusion. "Did what hurt?"

"When you broke both your arms so that you couldn't write or pick up the telephone?" His expression softened into a look of acceptance, and he nodded his head as if to say, "I get it." To his credit, he faced me head on.

"Let's go outside for a sec."

He led me out of the hotel and across the plaza to the steps of the church whose bell clanged every hour on the hour, reverberating through our hotel rooms. We sat down and, instead of looking at each other, watched all the shopkeepers hurrying home to dinner and electric taxis delivering guests to hotels and restaurants. A team of kids in their matching Adidas sweat suits burst out of the school doors after a game of volleyball and made their way noisily down the street. I broke the silence.

"So, I guess you're not asking me to the prom. I mean, if a ski racer ever got to go to a prom." He gave a little laugh, and I felt our personal bubbles start to dissolve. We were, after all, friends.

"I'm sorry Olivia. I really am. When I said I had fun that night I meant it. And I really do like you..."

"But not that way." I finished the sentence for him and we both let the words sit there. This time he broke the silence.

"I feel like you're more of a sister..." That was probably the second lamest line in the world, but he wasn't done.

"Can we still be..." I cut him off like a sushi chef with a Gin-su. "Just...don't...say it! Yes we can. But don't make me hear you say the lamest line in the world."

"Fair enough."

He might have left it at that, but he had to make it

worse by trying to make me feel better.

"You know, Eric really likes you." I gave an exasperated sigh.

"C'mon. He's younger than me. I like him too, but just…"

"As a friend?" This time he finished the lamest line in the world before it could come out of *my* mouth. I had to admit that he had me there.

"Doesn't it seem that whenever two people say they're 'just friends' it really means that one of them is bummed out about it?" I pondered.

"Yeah. It doesn't seem fair, does it? It reminds me of what my coach told me at my first Jr. Olympics when I fell in the last gate. 'Gravity is fair. Everything else is a bonus.' I guess it's the one thing you can always count on."

We stood up and walked back into the hotel together to join the rest of the group. As a consolation prize, he had his arm around my shoulders when we walked in. Nellie looked up and I thought I saw a sympathetic look, but then she looked away. I was that obvious I guess.

At 10:30 one of the boys looked at his watch and sounded the alarm: "Wheels up from the parking lot in 15 minutes!" They quickly gathered their things and made their way to the door in a pack.

Even though we could sleep in the next day, I woke up early and took my morning run. I loved that time of day when the streets were dark and empty and the only action was the electric bakery truck delivering fresh bread to the hotels. This morning, as I stretched my calves on the church steps, a strip of color caught my attention in the shadows; the back of a US Ski Team jacket that had emerged from the hotel's basement stairs and was moving briskly towards the parking lot. The walk looked familiar. The church bell broke the silence with six gongs, and he turned his head briefly so that I could see an unmistakable profile. It was Blake. But who had he been with? Anna? I was her roommate and, unless she pulled a real Ferris Bueller and created a human shaped lump in her bed that actually snored, I was pretty sure she was there all night, alone. Lucy! How many boyfriends did she really need? But it had to be Lucy.

Chapter 11:
Ho-Ho-Ho-Jo's
Christmas in November

A few snowflakes swirled around Nellie's VW Rabbit as she pulled in to Copper Mountain and parked in front of the main hotel check-in.

"Welcome to Fantasy Island!" I swept my arm across the expanse of the covered entryway, imitating white-suited Mr. Rourke, star of the second cheesiest television series in our memory; the one we had watched most every Saturday night of our young lives, right after *The Love Boat*, the cheesiest. "May I take your bags?"

She pointed to the two huge ski bags that were bending her roof racks. "They're all yours!"

"Tattoo!" I called out to nobody. "Where is that sidekick? Tattooooooo!"

"You're pathetic." It was great having Nellie back.

Copper Mountain felt practically like a dorm to us. We came here at least twice a year for this camp and for the National Championships later in the year. All the teams—men's and women's, speed and tech, A, B and C—

convened here for a final November tune-up before the season began. Then the World Cup teams, mostly A and B team athletes, headed directly to Europe while the C team went to their various races in the States. Anyone who didn't make that December trip to Europe would be considered a long shot to make the Olympic team so, for athletes "on the bubble," the time trials at Copper were important.

Nellie was supposed to qualify officially here, but her performance in Saas Fee had solidified her spot on the World Cup Team. When she had returned to school and told the coach she was dropping out effective immediately, he offered his genuine congratulations. In an Olympic year, nobody begrudged high aspirations however far-fetched they seemed. Before leaving home for this camp and six weeks on the road, I got a taste of just how much the Olympics validated our otherwise obscure pursuit.

"Do you think you're going to the Olympics?" Even my relatives couldn't help themselves from asking that question at a family gathering before I went to Colorado. I couldn't blame them. For the past six years I'd either missed Thanksgiving entirely or left right after it for a ski race. Now, with a few months until the Olympics, I was heading to Europe and missing another Thanksgiving. This time, however, nobody gave me any guilt about it. Instead, I got enthusiastic calls wishing me luck before I headed over to the opening races in Europe.

"They won't name the team until the end of January," I explained to everyone who called. When Luke called, I added what I was starting to believe:

"I'm pretty sure I have as good a chance as anyone."

"If you make it to Calgary, I'm coming to watch," he

promised.

"Will you be on TV?" my grandmother wanted to know.

"Maybe," I told her, hoping that was true. "If I have a really good race, I'll call so that you'll know to watch." My family was now conditioned to know what the timing of my calls from Europe meant. No call meant I'd done poorly. A call first thing in the morning, after they'd had their coffee but (hopefully) before they got the bad news on the hotline, meant I'd gotten injured. And a call in the middle of the night, made as soon as I got back to the hotel, meant I'd had a great race.

"Call anytime darling," my grandmother reminded me. "Collect!"

My uncle, whose insights were as humorous as they were astute, had some parting advice: "Just remember, Olivia. They all herd goats in the summer." It was his version of "they all put their pants on one leg at a time," a way of telling me not to be intimidated by the Europeans.

He was right because, although they didn't actually herd goats, most of the Europeans were destined to run the family business in their home villages. They might be farmers or butchers or hoteliers or bakers. Knowing they could step right back into their destined spot in a trade was like an insurance policy that let them risk everything on ski racing. Ski racing success, and the ability to open their own ski shop or hotel or local business with their winnings, could only sweeten their futures. Meanwhile, for us Americans, ski racing was a total gamble. We *might* win an Olympic medal, but even then the chances of ending up on a box of Wheaties were mighty slim. And, in the meantime, pursuing the dream led us further away from college, careers and anything else that mattered in our futures. I thought of that every time I talked to my friends from home, most of whom had already graduated from college. At least in an Olympic year, more people understood why I took the gamble.

Ken came out to greet Nellie. He smiled and gave her a big hug. "Great to see you!"

She kept her arms at her side and said nothing except, "Where do I park my car?" I was impressed at how she held her grudge. He deserved it all right but, still, it took an effort to keep hating someone so vigilantly.

When everyone had arrived, we reported in shifts to a big conference room filled with large cardboard boxes.

"Grab any big empty box," a US Ski Team employee instructed. An entire staff manned the US Ski Team's home office in Park City, but we rarely saw them. Mostly we spoke to them on the phone when an airline ticket hadn't arrived in the mail or a contract needed to be signed. It was nice to put faces with the voices on the phone, and they always seemed happy to connect with us, too. And "getting stuff" puts everyone in a good mood.

"A and B team gets one of every outerwear piece and whatever you need of everything else. C Teamers get the same except no one-piece suit or vest." After getting our instructions, I grabbed a box that looked like an oven could have fit in it, and started shopping.

Even though I was winning time trials on occasion, I was still just on the C Team. Nevertheless, within minutes my box was overflowing with a parka, warm-up pants, slalom pants, slalom sweater, two sweat suits, sweaters, turtlenecks, t-shirts, long underwear, socks, hats, gloves, snow boots and all kinds of samples from smaller sponsors. We had official snacks and handwarmers, lip balm, shampoo and, of course, official wind-tunnel approved hair mousse.

The vets like Natalie and Linda filled their boxes and left. The rookies unwrapped and tried on every uniform piece, chattering excitedly, modeling for each other and flinging tags and wrappers in all directions.

"Do you think I need smaller pants?"

"Doesn't this sweater look like something out of Star Wars?"

"Do you want to trade hats? I like the white one."

The rest of us tried on a few key pieces to make sure the sizing hadn't changed and squirreled away a few extras of anything that would make good Christmas gifts.

The only bummer this year was the color scheme. Athletes are, among other things, advertising tools, and the main priority for sponsors is visibility. This year our clothing sponsor had taken that quite literally and created uniforms in turquoise and bright orange.

"We look like we should be working at HoJos!" Jenna exclaimed as she surveyed the roomful of us in various uniform pieces. "May I take your order?"

"You might have thought they'd go with red white and blue, especially in an Olympic year," Anna remarked.

"Well, at least we won't get lost in the fog," I said, genuinely not concerned. Pathetic as it seemed, I couldn't help being excited every time I held up a piece of new clothing. I clearly remembered getting my very first piece of US Ski Team uniform as a thirteen-year-old when I swept my first Jr. Olympics. A US Ski Team "scout" had been there, hiding behind sunglasses and an upturned coat collar during the entire 5-day event. He never spoke to me but presented the coveted prize to me at the final awards banquet. At the time, I figured getting the rest of the uniform would be easy, and fast, but it had been very nearly impossible.

In the end, it took almost four more years to get my first full uniform. Jamie's had arrived at our house the same November day in a large box postmarked from Park City, UT. It wasn't just the uniform that had filled me with excitement. It was what it represented—the years of not getting a uniform and watching as others did, of failing at the Shootout and then coming so close every year but getting injured or passed up in favor of someone younger or thinner or better connected. Jamie had gotten his first US Ski Team uniform the previous year, so he let me cut the tape and peel open both flaps of cardboard.

Finally, finally, I saw it. *My* uniform. The one I feared I might never get. The thing that acknowledged I could compete on the world stage. Proof that I belonged. I tore open the plastic packages and laid it all out on the couch—the parka, warm-ups, vest, ski pants, sweater and silky smooth racing suit. The collection of slate blue clothing accented with white stripes and day-glo panels was not particularly attractive. But to me it was gorgeous. I tried each piece on carefully, treating it like expensive designer fashion. The uniform fit me perfectly and it was all mine.

My mother made us both pose in our uniforms on the porch. I complained but I loved it, and even three years later the "getting of the uniform" felt like a sacred rite. I still resented how easily some of the younger girls got them and envied the vets who kept track of their years on the team by the color of the uniforms. "That was the year we had navy blue. That was the gold and black year, etc." I fantasized about being there; at the place when I had raced so long on the World Cup that I lost track of the years.

The Copper camp wasn't all about getting our uniforms. There were the time trials, which continued to go well for me, and the ongoing task of fulfilling the Cheeseball's agenda. Less than a month before our first race, we devoted precious training hours to a media coach who suggested we wear "Nancy Reagan Red" at our interviews (as if we'd pack a little interview suit in our duffel bags) and taught us to respond to any question we hated with, "I'm glad you asked that question..." Contrary to the professional fashion advice (and any real sense of style) I wore a bright pink sweatshirt provided by my ski sponsor for my very first studio interview with Bob Beattie. As I hooked up the microphone and answered his questions under the spotlights I felt about four inches taller and very, very nervous.

Our press officer had tried to put us all at ease about being on camera by reminding us that, "Over a billion Chinese have never heard of any of you." Anna muttered to me under her breath, "And, thanks to you, neither have 240 million Americans."

She was right because, for the most part, the newspaper and TV reporters only cared about the stars. For the rest of us, they relied on the stats and one-liner summations that described each athlete in the hot-off-the-press media guides. Because of multiple injuries sustained in my younger years, I was known as the "Blue Cross Poster Child," while Anna's tennis skill and sheer strength made her the "power player," and Jenna's general lack of experience and caution made her the "fearless rookie." Each athlete had a tagline that, valid or not, was sufficient until somebody in the press had reason to dig deeper.

But going into an Olympic year, each reporter wanted to bank a reserve of inside scoop on the athletes with the best medal chances—veteran technician Natalie, the model-gorgeous superstar Donna and the spunky speedster Lucy. And they had a modest interest in the story value of the underdog, Nellie, a college girl who had come "out of nowhere" as they saw it. To think that this one-time sensation, who almost made the Olympic team at 17, was now such a surprise a mere four years later showed how little the mainstream press really knew about ski racing. Nellie could barely contain her annoyance when reporters used the term "out of nowhere." I saw her just after an interview in which she had obediently followed the expected script.

"How'd it go?" I asked when she got back to our room.

"You know. The usual. 'All I've ever dreamed about is a gold medal. My life's happiness depends on this'." She shrugged. "I gave them what they wanted." Off the record, she had a very different perspective on her "Olympic dream."

"I don't even care about getting a medal," she admitted to me after one interview. "I've put so much into this for so long. I just...I just want to go out on my terms. I don't want to get pushed out by an injury or a moron like Ken." Again, she seemed really stuck on Ken. I didn't love him by any stretch, but I'd gotten used to dealing with him. Sometimes I even liked him. It wasn't like her to let someone bug her so much.

"Can I ask you a question?"

"As long as it's not about my medal chances," Nellie joked.

"Why do you hate Ken so much? I mean *really* hate him?" Nellie stiffened a little, like she didn't want to go into it, but then she sat down on the couch.

"Got a few minutes?" she asked. I sat down across from her and listened.

"Do you remember Wayne from that dryland camp when I got hurt?" He was the football coach from CU that GI Jeff had recruited to 'toughen us up.' The rumor was that his mission was to try to bring each of us to tears, to work us that hard. We were supposed to hate him, and we did.

"Of course I remember him."

"Well I got to know him in Boulder, and he told me his side of the story."

She went on to recreate the scene on our last day of that camp, when all the coaches came down from their offices in Park City to observe a workout. First there were sprints up each set of stadium stairs, followed by track sprints, then agility exercises and "suicides"(a series of forward and backward sprints) on the field. Nellie was the only one who had not succumbed to tears once in the camp. I remember how the coaches applauded Nellie's toughness and ignored her occasional winces. If the doctor had issued restrictions, nobody was paying them any mind. I remember watching in awe and with a pang of jealousy.

After what we thought was our final round of knuckle push-ups on the searing hot track, Jeff called the girls over to where the coaches held heavy padded bags upright.

"We're running 40s with a twist because we have a little help today." He looked towards the row of coaches and went on to explain the drill.

"Run to the ten-yard line, cut right at 45 degrees and hit the bag. Hit it like you mean it, like you want to knock it into next week. Then run straight to the 20, cut left to the next bag. Same thing to the 30 and the 40. Hit, cut, and sprint as fast and as hard as you can. Two times through, then we're done. UNLESS, anyone slacks off. Then we do another round of stadiums."

That's when I went to the sidelines to get my jump rope. This was definitely something people with bad knees should avoid. I looked at Nellie to see if she was going to come with me, but she kept her head down, like she was ignoring me.

The girls took final sips from their water bottles and adjusted sweaty ponytails as they formed a line. Ken pulled Wayne aside and conferred with him about something.

"Lukovic! You first… Go!"

Wayne got behind the first bag and, as Nellie ran into it full force, instead of holding it in place he pushed hard against it. She never even had time to anticipate the impact of something twice her size coming at her full force. His 250 lb. frame was no match for her 120 lb. body and the tenuously rebuilt knee within it. Some people heard a pop, but everyone heard her scream and saw her crumple to the ground, grabbing her knee and rolling on the hot bristly turf.

The other girls instinctively rushed to her, but Jeff stopped them.

"Get back in line!"

He motioned to the coaches who were frozen in their spots not wanting to break ranks with Jeff but sharing the same impulse to rush forward.

"Help her up and get her some water."

Nellie was hauled away to the university's sportsmedicine clinic, where she got some painkillers and crutches. Before we could see her, she was back on a plane to Barton Memorial Hospital. Her season was over.

"I always blamed Wayne for it, for coming up against the bag like that, but it wasn't his fault. He knew it was a bad idea, and he didn't want to do it."

"Then why did he?"

"Because Ken *told* him to do it."

Suddenly all the bitterness I'd ever felt towards Ken returned, as raw anger. What had Jamie called him? A "weenie?" That was way too nice.

Nellie and Anna and I getting to room together was a rare treat. The technical team would travel separately from us to Europe. During the season, our paths would cross but usually only for a day or two with the technical specialists like Nellie. She was wise enough not to try speed events for a good long time on this comeback.

When we returned to the condo after dryland one afternoon, the red light on the phone was blinking. Anna, always anticipating a call from her boyfriend, picked up the message, and knitted her eyebrows like she was trying hard to understand something. She scribbled a number on a piece of paper and handed the phone to Nellie.

"It's for you. Crocodile Dundee I think, but I couldn't really understand what he was saying, mate. You'd better listen yourself." Nellie grabbed the phone and pressed a button to replay the message. She shook her head slightly and sighed, then pressed the 4 button to delete the message.

"Who was that?" We had to know when any guy called for one of us, but especially one with an accent.

"It's the coach of the Australian team...again."

"Why's he calling you?"

"He wants me to race in the Olympics for Australia." She said it as if he wanted her to dog-sit or do something equally mundane. "I guess they're bidding for a summer Olympics, so they're sort of desperate to show they're legitimate competitors in the Winter Games, too." Nellie's last name and dark skin came from her father, but her dual Australian citizenship came from her mother, an Aussie native. "The guy's relentless."

Anna gave me a look as if to check if I knew anything she didn't. I shrugged my shoulders and raised my eyebrows equally bewildered.

"Well that takes the guesswork out of it." Anna said. Did I detect a faint tinge of jealousy in her voice or was it my own? After all, how great would that be to just walk onto an Olympic team?

"You're going to do it, right?" Anna asked.

"Of course not!" Nellie looked at her in genuine surprise. "That would be like racing for the Virgin Islands or something. Totally lame!"

"It's not that bad. Australia's got some good racers, like Steven Lee and…"

"And Steven Lee," Nellie said. "They don't exactly have a women's team."

"Still, they have to start somewhere," I offered. "And besides, you've been through so much already. Everybody knows you deserve it, so does it really matter how you get there?"

Nellie's voice was low and flat. "Yeah. It does. If I'm not one of the best in the world, what's the point in going?"

"I hear you get a lot of cool stuff." Of course I was joking, sort of.

As much as we made fun of the frenzy of mainstream media hype, it was impossible not to get caught up in the excitement, to dream of what might happen if everything went right, if all our loose ends came together at the right time. Then, on one of the last days of training, Natalie caught a tip on a slalom gate and broke her ankle. I saw Dan in the lobby on his way back from the clinic and from giving several interviews. He looked horrible.

"What else can go wrong?" he asked to nobody in particular. If he only knew...

Chapter 12:
Me vs. the Goatherds

In late November, the grass was still green in Munich but, as we drove southeast, we started to see white on the peaks around Salzburg, Austria. Once off the Autobahn we passed signs for Altenmarkt, Schladming and Flachau, all familiar names from the racing circuit, then turned south to climb the unfamiliar turns of the Tauern Pass. The landscape got whiter and whiter until we stopped at the very top in the tiny winter wonderland town of Obertauern. This was one of Sepp's secret hideouts, and the family that owned and ran the *Tauernhof* hugged him and greeted us all warmly. We would be training here for five days before meeting up with the slalom team in Italy for our first World Cup.

It was my turn to room with Lucy and Rebecca, both of whom rated as "high-maintenance" roommates, especially when they were together. In addition to being competitive dieters and exercisers, Lucy sought constant attention, and Rebecca was a compulsive neat freak who brought her own mini cans of Lysol on every voyage. I took my time unloading my skis in the basement with

Steve. When I finally hauled my bags up to the third floor, Rebecca's clothes were neatly stacked, her facial cleansers, toners and lotions lined up in the bathroom, and she had disappeared to the fitness room. Lucy had already set up her bedside photo shrine. Her latest boyfriend, just out of the lake in his swim trunks, held a soaking wet dog and smiled at us from the frame. He was cute. They always were.

After I had set up my own shrine—my book, my lip balm and my journal—I was idly looking at the picture when Lucy popped up from a round of crunches and grabbed the frame.

"Wanna see something?" Before I could answer, she slid the photo up in the frame and revealed another picture behind it. In it she was dressed in a sleeveless gown, her buffed arms draped around the neck of a different guy—I'd even call him a man—dressed in a tuxedo.

"Who's that?" I asked, trying not to seem jealous or horrified even though I was a bit of both. There wasn't anything wrong with her having an older boyfriend. She was 23 after all. But how many did she need? And what was wrong with dog boy? He looked like more fun to me. Lucy smiled proudly at the picture.

"That's Roland. Isn't he gorgeous?"

"Is he...I mean, is this...for real?" I dodged her question about his appearance. Roland just looked like he was trying too hard.

"Totally for real. He has a Porsche!" OK, well, that explained it. Curtains for dog boy. I was still digesting Lucy's layers of boyfriends when Rebecca burst through the door. She looked flushed and flustered.

"What happened to you?" Lucy asked.

Rebecca took a few moments to compose herself.

"I just saw Sepp in the sauna."

"So?"

"I mean I *saw* Sepp, like, all of him."

Lucy and I must have cringed at the same time. Then we started laughing at the vision of Rebecca walking in on Sepp taking a sauna the European way, buck-naked. Some of the saunas even had signs outside them with a bathing suit and a red line crossed through it, as if wearing a bathing suit might get you arrested.

"It's no big deal, " I assured her. "When you see him at dinner, just say 'Ich habe dich gesehen,' because you really did." Lucy howled at the uniquely appropriate German translation for "I have seen you," and for a second I thought Rebecca was going to burst into tears.

"It's not funny!" she insisted, her cheeks reddening. Suddenly her face relaxed as she admitted, "Ok, it wasn't pretty, but I guess it *was* funny."

For the next four days, we trained downhill next to the Austrian men's team, the gods of Alpine skiing. Franz Klammer, my hero in 1976, had recently retired, but other stars had taken his place. Easily ten of them could win a World Cup on any given day but, like every other country, only four Austrians could race in an Olympic event. Every training run became a full-on race. Even here, in a place that looked like Whoville on the summit of nowhere, these athletes handled themselves like rock stars, fending off autograph seekers who hounded them, flirting shamelessly with all of us once we got on the tram, but mostly with Lucy who egged them on. Meanwhile their coaches, whose jobs depended on Olympic medals, chain-smoked cigarettes by the side of the course. If they were this nervous in November, I could only imagine how stressful their season was going to be.

Sepp, comparatively, was chilled out. Some of the girls weren't happy with his direct coaching style

"He told me I skied like his Oma," Rebecca sulked one time, and she was not comforted when I assured her his grandmother probably skied pretty well. But his minimalist approach made me feel confident, like he had faith in us. Plus, I'd learned not to trust the talkers. They usually delivered the least wisdom in the most words.

At the bottom of the course, I did see Sepp talking casually with one of the Austrian coaches, and both of them nodded in my direction. I thought I heard him say "Heisse Scheisse," and then he winked at me. He was either telling the other coach I was "the hot shit" or that he had the runs. I thought I knew which. I hoped I knew.

The family that ran the hotel practically adopted us. From the time we arrived, they set about finding ingredients for a proper Thanksgiving dinner, complete with two turkeys and preiselbeeren—berries that could be turned into something like cranberry sauce. On Thanksgiving morning, we took over the hotel kitchen to make stuffing, apple pies, mashed potatoes and Rebecca's low-fat banana bread that looked like sculpted dirt.

While the turkeys roasted, we turned on the TV to watch the opening slalom broadcast live on Eurosport from Italy. The first American up was Donna. Without Natalie, she was our best technical skier and was skiing her best ever. Since those World Championships Nellie and I had watched bitterly from the couch in Hotel California three years earlier, we had seen the hopes for the future of the US Ski Team shift entirely from Nellie to Donna.

With her "All-American" looks—thick blonde hair

and a smile that flashed brightest for the camera—"Madonna" had her own fan club in Europe and was the only skier who had become a household name in the States. As teammates, we respected all that Donna had accomplished and the fact that she had reached beyond the ski world to raise awareness for our sport. But we also knew the less attractive side of America's sweetheart, the side that always nabbed the best seat in the van or the one single room, saw nothing wrong with jumping into a hot bath that somebody had drawn for themselves and never went to anyone else's awards ceremony ("I've got my own medals to win"). But, so far, she had delivered for her fans with the help of many factors, including her legendary confidence, deliberate undertraining and plain good luck. Not counting the traumas she faked to get out of dryland camps or training and her multiple mysterious "overuse" injuries, she had never been injured. That alone was a huge advantage over most of us, especially considering she now had three full years on the World Cup under her belt.

In every interview, Donna was intense and focused with neither a hair nor a sponsor's logo out of place. Like Lucy she thrived on the limelight, but she never let anything or anyone get in the way of her mission. If a sponsor appearance or an interview encroached on her rest time, she'd just blow it off. And if there was a guy in her life, and there always was, you could be sure he was not calling the shots. As the season approached, her polish had hardened into an edge, and even her occasional fun streak had disappeared. Everyone deals with pressure her own way and hers was to greet it with laser focus. The coaches, the athletes and the press all knew that this was her time. She was coiled and ready to spring.

We clustered chairs around the TV and got in position, excited to watch her burst out of the gate. The racer before her caught an edge and mowed down a gate near the bottom of the hill. There was a brief hold while courseworkers armed with giant augers converged, one drilling out the broken gate to replace it with a new one and others fixing various gates that seemed loose or askew. When Donna appeared in the start house we shouted at the TV:

"C'mon Donna!" "Charge it all the way!" "Get after it girl!"

She blasted out of the gate. We cheered when her first split time flashed on the screen. At the second split, she was again well in the lead. Then, five gates from the finish, a course worker stood directly in her line, waving his arms. It was like a big game of chicken, and Donna never lost those. Unflinching, she held her line straight at him. At the last moment he scurried out of the way, and Donna disappeared in a puff of snow. It was as if something had yanked her down to the ground. We could hear her scream and when the snow settled, we saw her writhing wildly, pointing to her ski boot. Before the crowd of coaches and race workers converged on her, we could just make out the top handle of a metal auger sticking out of the snow where the waving man had been standing. It had stopped her foot instantly. One of our coaches made a sound like he'd just been kicked in the stomach; for a long time nobody spoke.

Later that day, we sat down to Thanksgiving dinner. Everyone managed to pull out something fresh and nice to wear, and Anna produced an entire outfit for the occasion. We were still somber when Sepp, in his coat and tie, made a toast. "We can be thankful for our health and we send our prayers to Donna. We can be thankful for the hard work and talent that has gone into this team and for the opportunity to work together. I am proud of you all." He paused. "And we can be thankful that I went into the kitchen while you were all getting fancied up, and made sure there was plenty of butter in the mashed potatoes. Stupid diets!"

With the mood lightened, we dug into the most delicious Thanksgiving meal I'd ever had. Late that night I went down to the reception desk and called my grandmother's house in Sacramento, where the entire extended family was gathering for their feast. They passed the phone around so that everyone could wish me luck.

My grandmother got on the line at the end of the call and asked me again when I would be on TV. I assured her I'd try my best to do something TV-worthy, and she offered some advice that I suspect few downhillers ever get: "Don't let them make you do anything you don't want to do, because you're precious."

I held back a giggle as I envisioned explaining my preciousness to the coaches but promised her just the same. After I hung up, I realized that even half a world away from my family, I felt completely at home. My teammates and coaches and reps were now a family. By the time we packed our gear, loaded the vans and hugged our hotel family goodbye the next day, our mood and excitement had rebounded. The season was about to begin.

I staked my claim in Steve's car. We were headed south to the Italian border, then across Italy on a stretch of Autobahn known as the black tongue route because of all the coffee drivers tend to gulp down at rest stops along the way. It was going to be a long journey, so I wanted to be able to fully relax and not worry about editing anything I said. Driving with Steve wasn't like driving with Dan. We didn't talk about *War and Peace*. Instead we ate beef jerky and traded gossip about who among the other racers and reps was dating whom. And Steve never tried to hit on any of us. "Ski racer chicks are not my type, " he often reminded me. "I prefer girls whose legs are smaller than mine and at least *sometimes* let me be right."

I told him about my current fascination with *Edie* a book about the rapid rise and ruination of a pop star who was starting to remind me of Lucy.

"But what's your boyfriend Dan making you read?" Steve joked. Sort of joked is more like it, but I didn't mind it from him.

"*Les Miserables*. It sort of seems like a good name for our team this year."

"Don't say that!" Steve's sharp, almost harsh tone took me by surprise.

"You can't afford to get down on yourself. Of course you want to be faster. I want you to be faster and so do the coaches, the Trustees, the sponsors, the press— everyone with skin in this game. But just wanting a gold medal isn't enough. It's all got to come together, and you're not in control of everything. Plus, it's only your first full season on the World Cup. Take it easy—Rome wasn't built in a day."

I liked Steve's advice much better than what I usually got from Ken. "Pressure makes diamonds," he liked to say. Maybe so, but it hadn't necessarily brought out the best in us so far. Thanks to Steve, his classic rock and the stash of *People* magazines sent over by his girlfriend, I felt totally relaxed when we pulled in to Sestriere.

Walking into the hotel felt like entering a thick dark

cloud. The tech skiers were all milling around outside the dining room, having just finished their meeting. One girl shlumped across the lobby in her sweats, looked up at us, nodded "Hey" and kept moving to the elevator. She looked tired and sort of spaced out, like we usually looked at the end of January but not at the beginning of the season. Donna's rep, whose top athlete was now Greta, had just returned from Torino where he had visited Donna in the hospital. She was waiting there, alone, until the swelling in her ankle went down enough for surgery. Dan looked relieved to be done with the team meeting and came over to greet us.

"How was the trip?" he asked, trying to smile, then directed us to the front desk. "The rooming list is here. Sharpie, I moved you into Donna's room with Monica. As soon as you all move in, let's meet back here. I'll give you tomorrow's schedule and we can have dinner."

Nellie sprang up from behind me and pushed my hat over my eyes. I was still surprised every time I saw her back with us after nearly a year off snow.

"I just got chocolate chip cookies from home," she whispered, making sure Greta didn't hear her. "Meet me in my room after dinner." Ever since their marathon trip to Saas Fee, Greta had become dependent on Nellie.

"She's like Lyme disease," Nellie had complained at one point. "She starts out like an annoying little itch and then you're stuck with her for a year."

When I got my bags to the room, Monica was on the phone with her boyfriend. The dreaded boyfriend calls. I hated listening to those. But she looked up and twirled her finger in the air to show she was wrapping it up, so I stayed.

"Yeah, I know," she said, her voice totally flat. "But

these last two months already feel like they're going to take forever. I can't *wait* to be done...Call me tomorrow?... Thanks, me too. Yeah, bye." She hung up.

"Hey there. It's all yours now," she said, pointing to the empty bed.

With Donna gone, Monica was the sole survivor of the Fabulous Four from the Shootout six years earlier, the trial that was supposed to identify the top prospects for Calgary. It sounded like she wasn't going to be around for much longer. Over the years, as she watched her teammates on the technical team get ousted, she and the "upstart" Donna had forged an unlikely bond of survivorship. Donna's self-confidence buoyed Monica, while Monica's overriding calm anchored Donna. Without Donna, Monica must have felt pretty alone.

"Are you really quitting?" I blurted out. Normally I pretended I hadn't heard any of the boyfriend calls, but I was too shocked to let the editor upstairs in my head kick in. Monica didn't seem to mind though.

"I guess I wasn't really sure about it until Donna got hurt. But, yeah, I'm quitting.

"But why? You're, like, the second best ranked skier in the country in three events, right? You're totally there. You can't quit now!"

"It took a lot out of me to get here. And now? I don't know. I just don't want it anymore. It's fine on the good days, but I'm not having many of those. And on the bad days, it's all I can do to even get in the gate and go for it."

I knew plenty about bad days when it was cold and you had PMS or were a little sick and were on a course that was just a little too hairy and you wanted to crawl back into bed. But those were all part of the sport. We'd all been there, and we got through them.

She continued: "All I ever wanted was to get to the Olympics, and now that I have a shot I'm not even that psyched. It's hard for me to explain because I can't really understand how I got here. One minute I'm the next great thing, and then I'm 24, too old even to race for college and too burnt out to do this. I just know I'm done."

Monica having "a shot" at the Olympics was an understatement. Given the shape of our team, I figured she could ski backwards and still qualify.

"So, if, I mean, *when* you make the team, are you even going to go?" I couldn't believe I was even asking the question, but suddenly I really wondered.

"Duh—of course!" Monica burst out with a little laugh. "I'm conflicted but I'm not *stupid*. It's the Olympics after all, and you never know…"

Suddenly I felt the urge to get out of the hotel, fast, before the downer vibes sucked all my energy. Instead of heading to the dining room after our meeting, I darted out of the hotel. Once I was beyond the hotel lights, I felt my whole body relax. I slowed down and looked up at the huge starry sky that felt like it might swallow me whole if I reached high enough and stood on my tiptoes. Wind blew a veil of snow, like little grains of sand, over the pavement, and the mountains rose high on either side of the road. Far to the left, I could see the Super G finish all lit up. I followed the slope upwards with my eyes, as it disappeared around a corner and into the trees.

Without thinking I walked towards the race hill, skirting the bright finish area in the shadows, and started walking up the hill. I had to keep to the side of the trail to get traction in the softer snow. I climbed up, around the first corner and then another, until the only light came from the stars and the only sound came from my steps crunching in the snow. I looked up, took a long breath of the mountain air, and thought about Donna, the great Madonna, all alone in her hospital room with her shattered ankle and her shattered dream, under the same sky. Where was Team Donna now? Her script, it had seemed, was all but written. This was supposed to be Donna's year. But one moment can change everything.

The next morning, we loaded the vans early and rushed to the warm-up area on a tiny crowded Poma that all the teams shared. I had just reached the front of the line when a Swiss girl tried to elbow past me. Without thinking, I pushed back and scooted ahead of her. When I looked back to catch the Poma, I recognized the girl I'd cut off. I'd last seen her face smiling at me from a yogurt advertisement on a giant billboard along the Autobahn. I had just bossed myself past Maria Walliser, the pride of Switzerland.

After a few runs, we piled back into the vans and headed to the chairlift for inspection. I had planned to take my usual long, careful inspection, pausing where the other girls paused, to look like I knew what I was doing. Inspection in Super G is even more important than in downhill because you don't get any training runs to figure out the line, the speed and how much air you'll catch off the jumps. You get one shot to look at it and then it's race time. As soon as I started down the course, I became aware of a serious problem. I had to pee desperately, and the course was lined top to bottom with two high rows of orange plastic fencing. Worse yet, television cameras were poised on platforms all the way down the hill. There was no way to escape for a pit stop in the trees. Besides, I was still on the C team, so this brand new race suit was the only one I had. I couldn't compromise it with a trip into the prickly woods on its very first day.

I made the closest thing I could to an "Austrian inspection," which is a high speed side-slip through the gates. A true Austrian inspection—when you ski the course while looking at it—is totally illegal and grounds for disqualification, so I made a series of skids, barely looking at the course and not even stopping to talk to the coaches. Nobody could mistake it for a strategy. At the bottom, I clicked out of my skis and ran down the street all the way to the hotel bathroom. Then I raced back out to the chairlift, weaving through the gathering crowd. Amidst the finish area commotion, I managed to get on the wrong chairlift and had to tear down the hill one more time to get on the right chairlift. I arrived at the top of the course with just ten racers to go before my start, cutting it close but not stressfully so. Sean helped me strip off my warm-ups and parka as I ran through the course with my eyes closed. I knew it, sort of. Trust your instincts, I told myself. Even with the scramble, I felt strangely calm. Usually this was when I crammed my mind with technical reminders and advice from the coaches. Today, I remembered my promise to Dan and the weight of regret at the finish line in Vail. I did not want to feel that way again. Only one thing stuck in my head: "Release the hounds!"

Sean brought me the radio for my course report from the coaches.

"All set?"

I nodded and he gave my shoulders one last squeeze before his inspirational parting advice: "Remember the Alamo—they lost, they died!"

I blasted out of the start and attacked the course just

like I had attacked every training course all summer and fall. It felt easy, maybe too easy, and I wondered if it was because I was going slowly. That happens all too often in speed events. You think you had an amazing run because it felt so perfect, so controlled. But it feels that way because you are crawling over the terrain instead of skipping over it. Near the bottom I swung wide on a gate, traveling extra distance, but instead of jamming to recover I let me skis run out and eased my way back onto the right line. Bummer, I thought. It felt pretty good until then. I had hoped to maybe, finally, crack the top 20 in Europe, where it counted.

I tucked through the finish and heard the crowd roar. Usually all I got, at best, were a few polite cowbell rings when I crossed the line. The first person I saw in the crowd before coming to a stop was Gus, smiling from outside the finish fence. He was holding up six fingers. It took me a bit to register, but then I turned around to see the scoreboard with a big number 6 lit up next to my name and broke into a huge smile. The camera man swung around and closed in on me, so I waved into his lens. Before I left the finish corral, Bob Beattie caught up to me, smiling like he always did.

"Olivia! Great run—can we ask you a few questions?" Bob Beattie asking *me* for a post-race interview. This still felt like a movie. My rep handed me a fresh pair of skis, and Todd appeared to make sure the brand name on the pair of goggles around my neck was visible. Bob congratulated me and asked a few questions about the course.

"Did you know coming down that you were going to have a good run?"

I thought about it for a second and realized that

something *had* felt different, and easier, than any other World Cup race.

"I kind of knew it all morning. I felt totally relaxed when I woke up this morning and, uh, I had a good inspection…"(I lied) "…I wasn't thinking of much in the course except going fast. I just felt good today. It didn't feel like anything special."

"Well, that's pretty good for nothing special."

"Yeah, I'll take it!" then added, "that or five places better." Where did that little shot of swagger come from? Bob laughed and wished me luck in the next races.

As I made my way outside the finish corral Anna and Nellie nearly bowled me over, each giving me a hug and a high five. Lucy and Greta were already long gone. I heard someone say: "Congratulieren" and looked up to see a pretty dark haired racer in a Swiss parka. Maria Walliser extended her hand to mine, and I took it. "Danke!"

My smile stayed there as I walked slowly back to the hotel. Along the way, coaches and reps from other teams shook my hand, and the ones I knew hugged me. Kids swarmed me—"Autogram! Autogram!"—holding out cards and pieces of clothing for me to sign. They pleaded with every racer exiting the finish corral, but this time they followed me. The Toddler was leading two German men towards me, the big bosses from my goggle company. "Congratulieren," one then the other said, giving me a kiss on each cheek and shaking my hand. "Please, take this, and this." They handed me a bright pink umbrella and a fedora cap with the company logo. I'd seen Maria Walliser wearing one like it.

"Danke Schon!" I said, smiling.

"She could use a new sweatsuit," Todd added from nowhere.

"Ja, naturlich," one man answered, still smiling.

"And actually I could use one, too..." The Toddler was nothing if not opportunistic.

"Es kommt sofort." The man assured us. Right away. It's all coming right away. In so many ways, it felt like that.

As soon as I got to the hotel, I called home in what was the middle of the night for them. My mother answered and when she heard my voice, her grogginess turned to alarm.

"Olivia. Oh, Livvie! Are you all right? Did you get hurt?"

"No! I'm fine, I'm really fine. I'm in Italy, and...and I finally did it!"

Chapter 14:
Another One Bites the Dust

Like I said, one moment—or if you're a ski racer, a minute and a half—can change everything. Before I pushed out of the start in Sestriere, I was just another hack, wondering when, or if, I'd ever break through. Ninety seconds later, I was *somebody*. By the time we showed up at the top of our first downhill in Val D'Isere, France, coaches, reps, athletes and officials, who had never before noticed me, greeted me by name. It's not like I felt any better than I was before, but I did feel a huge sense of relief. This working hard and never giving up thing, it seemed, might actually work.

Some of my teammates hadn't experienced this revelation. Others like Lucy and Anna had been there but badly needed a refresher. Already, even before our first downhills of the season, we felt like we were behind. It was as if each injury—Linda's then Natalie's and finally Donna's—knocked us down from wherever we had climbed. Our only victory over the Europeans came when we smuggled Greta across the border from Italy to France. She had forgotten her passport at the hotel in

Sestriere. It was too far to go back, and the technical team had left the hotel before us to get to some Europa Cups in Switzerland. Apparently leaving her at the border wasn't an option, so we buried her beneath a few huge ski bags in the cargo van and drove through customs nervously. Sometimes the bored-looking men in military gear just looked through the stack of passports and waved us through, but other times they were looking for a little action.

We stayed quiet and gave our best, innocent smiles but the guard peered into the back of the van and asked Dan to open it. He pulled one ski bag aside and revealed the tip of Greta's glove.

All of us froze...except Lucy, who bounced up to the guard, tapped his shoulder and pleaded ugently, "Ou est le, uh, twaah-LETTE?" He shrugged his shoulders, pointed to the woods and gestured to the other guard to close the van doors.

Our hearts were still pounding when we stopped in the next town to uncover Greta and revive her with hot cocoa and high fives. The fugitive seemed downright giddy.

I had never raced in Val D'Isere and hadn't even watched the race on TV last year because I was so mad that Sepp left me behind. "There's no rush," he had assured me. "You'll be better off starting your downhill comeback in the States." He had explained that it was Ken's idea to send so many rookies to Val D'Isere "for experience" and, that if it were up to him, most would have stayed in the States with me. I was insanely jealous of all the other girls who made that December trip to Europe, but Sepp was right. By February I was in a luxurious Swiss hotel in Crans Montana, getting foil-wrapped chocolates on my pillow every night, while most of them were fending off dust bunnies on the Balkan Tour.

Now I enjoyed taking in Val D'Isere for the first time. The streets were alive, strung with Christmas lights and full of people in all stages of holiday cheer. Pop and country music blared from cafes and trendy boutiques. (Along with their innate sense of style many of the French seem to share a secret cowboy alter-ego). Huge crowds clogged the narrow main street and clustered around street carts selling fresh roasted chestnuts and jam-filled crepes.

The men kicked off their downhill racing season here, too, so we visited them at their hotel on the other side of town. We joined them for a fondue dinner where, according to tradition, you "must" kiss the person on your right if the bread falls off your narrow fondue fork and into the pot. I noticed that Blake kept angling to sit next to Rebecca while Lucy kept scootching her chair next to his. I was not about to save him but enjoyed watching the scene. If anything had happened between he and Lucy in Saas Fee, he clearly wanted to put it behind him. Eventually he gave up and used a big dinner fork to keep hold of his bread.

Most of the time I talked to Eric. It was his first trip to Val D'Isere, too, and he couldn't wait to get on the course. "I just want to go fast!" was his standard refrain when asked about his immediate or long term future. Beyond making the Olympic team, his main goal for the year was to race the Hahnenkamm and shed the Rookie Rock. Just thinking of the Hahnenkamm made me happy to be a girl and never have to run that thing. After dinner we exchanged movie stashes and whatever gossip from home we each had, then left the boys to their own space.

Off the hill I loved Val D'Isere. On the hill, the downhill—like every downhill the first time I saw it—sort of freaked me out. I much preferred Super G's all-or-nothing one-run format, featuring all the speed and excitement of downhill without the anxiety of training days. I rarely slept the night before running each new downhill course, but by race day I had usually worked up my confidence enough to be firing all guns. I was getting used to this process, starting to trust it and losing slightly less sleep. But still, the routine was exhausting.

The Val D'Isere downhill made me especially nervous because the one time I'd watched it on TV, an Austrian girl had almost died after flinging herself into the giant orange netting with so much force that she bounced back and slammed onto the icy trail. On our first inspection, I couldn't help replaying the crash in my mind when I got to that section near the bottom of the course. It was this course's "tuna turn," a long, net-lined right hand sweeper through a high-speed compression. The team's sports psychologist was supposed to help us with things like my first run anxiety, my tuna turn fixation and the niggling question on all of our minds: who's going down next? By now we all knew those confessions went straight to the coaches, so we kept them to ourselves. But at times like this, when I stood there contemplating a massive orange safety net while wondering how I'd make it through the next few hours let alone days, I seized on any sign of comfort. As if on cue, a country western song blared through the course speakers just then, and the lyrics made me smile: "Good ain't forever and bad ain't for good..."

A bitter cold front had moved across Europe, making the short, dark December days even colder than usual.

Under the circumstances, "warm-up" was a misnomer for the purpose of a morning jog, but I liked to keep it in my routine. In the pre-dawn of the first race day, I ended up on the same route as Anna towards the outskirts of the village. After only a few minutes running beside each other in silence, we paused where the narrow path ended with a fence at the foot of an icy meadow that shone in the moonlight. Our eyelashes were coated with frost, and our toes were frozen hard in our running shoes. I managed to free my mouth from under my scarf, jacket collar and turtleneck and bring it as close to the surface as I dared.

"What are you thinking about right now?" Long pause, then in a voice tinged with shame:

"UC San Diego."

We weren't yet two races in to the season.

This year Val D'Isere lived up to its sometimes nickname, Val M'Isere. At least for the Americans it did. There would be no call home. A Swiss girl my age—one I had easily beaten in my first Europa Cup downhill— won her first World Cup. Like a big family, the younger Swiss athletes were maturing under the guidance and shelter of their more accomplished teammates. Our decidedly less nurturing environment was breeding a family of cannibals. The athletes were starting to snip at each other, the reps talked amongst themselves about the coaches being clueless and the coaches blamed our disappointing results largely on our equipment. When that got back to the reps, they bristled.

"So now it's our fault!" Lucy's rep Drew, who endured his share of abuse, was livid as he packed up his ski tuning bench and slammed his tools into a giant metal box. It wasn't fair really. A big reason why Lucy was slow was because there was less of her to build momentum and maintain it. But she was our top racer, so people had to point their fingers at someone else and that someone was Drew. I followed Steve outside, carrying one end of an enormous ski bag and hefting it into the back of his car. Steve still managed to smile despite whatever had gone down in the ski room.

"I've always heard there are three great things about France." He slammed down the hatch and finished his thought.

"Wine, cheese, and leaving."

From Val D'Isere we drove four hours to the little Swiss village of Leukerbad, a high-altitude, old world retreat that is famous for its therapeutic baths. We arrived at the hotel after dark to a chilly reception from the proprietors who were the exact opposite of our Obertauern hosts. The Swiss, in general, crave perfect order. These Swiss hoteliers understandably preferred their older, quiet, well-dressed clientele with thick wallets, to a young energetic team with piles of gear who exercised in the hallways and only spent money on phone calls home.

The next morning, as I was leaving the hotel for my pre-dawn jog, I noticed a suspicious lump in the middle of the still-dark hallway. Remembering the large German Shepherd I'd seen the night before, I walked way around it. When I returned from my run, I noticed the lump had been disturbed ever so slightly. At breakfast Lucy was quick to remark on the gross deposit.

"Did you see that dog poop?" she asked the table. Jenna had been unusually quiet until now. Most mornings she made a noisy entrance, greeting everyone in a variety of languages, throwing her energy at people so forcefully that they nearly spit out their coffee. Sometimes it made me smile and other times it annoyed me.

"See it?" asked Jenna rhetorically. "Last night I thought I dropped my glove in the hall, so this morning when I saw something lying in the middle of the floor I reached down to pick it up…"

"You did not!" Lucy broke out into one of her loud cackles and the rest of the table started cracking up. We hadn't laughed together in far too long, and now it was as if Jenna's mishap had broken a dam. The Canadian team all gave us dirty looks as if we were a bunch of misbehaving children, and the hotel owner scowled at us from behind the bar, but still we couldn't stop. We needed this laughter like oxygen.

The downhill didn't look particularly fearsome during inspection, but there was so little snow that even sideslipping you could feel every little rock, roll and ditch underfoot. Plus, except for the top three gates, the entire course was in the shadows. My first run felt more like a jerky, pounding rodeo ride than a downhill. Sometimes a really tough course sharpens your concentration, demands your best skills and makes you rise to the challenge. The problem with Leukerbad was that it was completely uninspiring. There was no fast section, no series of tough turns, no big jump. It just felt like rollerskating really fast down a bumpy road on metal wheels. I'd never run a course like it. In the ongoing tug-of-war between my inexperience and my enthusiasm, inexperience was winning.

On race day, Jenna and I both fell less than halfway down. Jenna's crash was spectacular, as usual, with tumbling, broken gates and flying skis. Watching Jenna's all-or-nothing approach reminded me of my first season on the Nor Am circuit—the top level of competition in the States. That year I crashed hard nearly every race but dusted myself off without complaint and went right back up for another run as if to say, "Thank you sir, may I have another?" Any hesitation to get back on the horse, however justified, might have been the end of my career, so I survived that year on ice packs and Advil. Jenna's rookie season happened to be on the World Cup in an Olympic year, so her crashes were high speed and usually on TV. Commentators loved her. Fortunately, she was tough enough to keep coming back for more.

My sit-and-spin fall was more of a surrender. Even after three training runs, I had no clue how to ski the course and was jealous of all the Swiss who had raced here many times. I wished for someone who could tell me how to attack this course and, even with my limited German, tried to eavesdrop on the Swiss course reports that came through on their radios. I really wanted to live until Christmas...or at least until the Super G.

Back in the hotel, a cold war was brewing between us and the Canadian team. Damn those Canadians. Even the ones my age, who couldn't manage to crack the top 40 in Europa Cups two years earlier (much to our entertainment), were now regularly poking into the top 15 in World Cups. Their team was anchored by three older vets—two of whom were already married—who set a subdued tone. All of them acted a solid ten years older than us. They thought we made too much noise which, as a team, we did. The hoteliers agreed with the Canadians, especially because we had purchased a big stash of Schladmingers while driving through Salzburg. "Schladis" were little green bombs about the size of a pinky finger with a match head on one end and the time-delayed bang of an M-80 firecracker. You could strike them casually and drop them anywhere. We usually only used them on each other while skiing, but Jenna threw one off her porch, and it landed much too close to a Mercedes returning from the spa. This did not help our reputation.

The night after the downhill and before the Super G, we had our usual team meeting. Up until now, Ken had let Sepp and Dan run their respective team meetings. But now that it was becoming very clear that they weren't going to be able to recreate the dream team of '84, Ken felt it was his duty to "take charge" with more of his inspirational speeches. When he stood before us, holding up a sheet of paper, I noticed that his normally green eyes were black. That couldn't be good.

"See this?" He held the paper out to us. "This is the Nations Cup standings." The Nation's Cup is awarded at the end of the World Cup season to the country whose athletes score the most World Cup points. The Austrians, with their bottomless talent pool, usually took it by hundreds of points, so we never set out to win it. Nevertheless, it is a barometer by which to judge a national team's progress, or lack thereof.

"Forget about the Swiss, Germans and Austrians," Ken continued. "The French are ahead of us, the Canadians, the Yugoslavians…" He went down the list, finishing with, "the *Litchensteinians!*" That hurt considering their entire team included one racer. The lecture got harsher with Ken pretty much implying that we were, a) quitters, and b) wimps.

I was still riding the remnants of my wave of confidence from Sestriere, so I mistook this for a pep talk, or at least a well-deserved kick in the pants. But when it was over, the room went silent. I looked around and saw bowed heads and red eyes. Sepp was avoiding eye contact with anyone. He looked mad, but I couldn't tell if he was mad at us or at Ken. Anna looked especially upset. It reminded me of how bummed out she used to get when Ken or Trent got on her case about her weight, but this time she was inconsolable.

The next day everyone had shaken "the talk," except Anna. I tried to find her after breakfast, but she had disappeared and headed to the lifts alone. After inspection, she and Lucy headed to the start while I warmed up in the lodge at the top of the mountain with Jenna and Rebecca. I watched the first few racers on TV then skied down to the start. I had barely gotten there when racer #20 backed out of the gate, and her trainer put a parka over her shoulders. Course hold. Bummer. I had timed my arrival just right, but now I'd have to wait in the cold instead of in the lodge and I was annoyed. Then came the whop, whop, whop of a helicopter airlifting a racer from the lower part of the course. I ignored it by concentrating on my run and was so focused that I didn't even notice when Sean disappeared from the start and sped down the course.

Twenty minutes later, I pushed out of the gate for an ugly but reasonably fast run. The course bucked me all over the place but, after the previous day's performance and the quitter scolding, I had decided to fight back with Jamie's standard advice and "go down swinging." I quickly found our radio in the finish bag and radioed an upbeatish course report to the girls in the start. Only then did I notice Howard Nicks and Lucy standing together, their faces ashen. Howard had his long arm around Lucy's shoulder and looked as if he might be ill.

Finally, I put it together. Anna was missing. The helicopter had been for her. I ran over to Howard and Lucy and they described what had happened, how Anna had swung wide on the second to last gate. When it was obvious she wasn't going to make the last gate, she could have let off her edge and missed it. But Anna didn't quit, couldn't quit. It was her streakness and, quite nearly this time, her fatal flaw. Instead of letting up, she bore down harder on the skis, cranking them until she barely made the gate with all her weight back over her tails. Just past the gate, her skis crested a roll that swept her feet out from underneath her. She was still airborne, her body extended sideways when she wrapped herself around a steel finish post at 60 miles per hour. Lucy had seen the whole thing and was still in shock.

When Rebecca finished and came over to me, I started to tell her about Anna. "I know," she interrupted. Even though she was breathing hard from her run, her face had no color. "Jenna and I were in the lodge. We saw the whole thing on TV."

Anna was flown to a hospital at the base of the valley in Sion, where she underwent emergency surgery, first to repair her broken femur and stop the blood loss. Later, when that was under control, they would deal with her broken pelvis, broken back and blown out knee. In all, she was lucky to survive, lucky that we were close to a modern hospital and that the doctor with us on that trip was one of the best. As bad as it was, things could have been much worse.

We saw Anna later that evening when she was barely conscious, hooked up to a respirator, IV's and an array of beeping, flashing machines. A couple of days later, we returned on our way to the airport. By then, she had regained her humor, if not her sense.

"I still want to know my time," she insisted. "I know I broke the timing light... along with everything else."

It was a quiet ride to Geneva. I thought about how much we were going to miss Anna individually and as a team. She was one of our top athletes, but she was also the mortar that kept us together. Even when she was down on herself, Anna would find a way to make us laugh. When things got frosty within the group, she always knew how to break the ice or, her specialty, how to blow off steam. I didn't know for sure, but I suspected each of us in that crappy, icicle-dripping van was digesting the loss and facing a truth we'd been trained to ignore. Ski racing is dangerous. At this level, every time we got into the gate, no matter how strong and good and well prepared we were, we risked something. Some days it was just our pride, and other days, without warning, it was much more. We all knew that—but now we felt it in our guts.

Chapter 15:
Countdown to Calgary

"Happy New Year!"

Nellie was kicking me on the floor of the airplane where I had fashioned a comfortable nest out of the airline blanket and my ski parka. 1988 started in a familiar way for me, with a seat on the Screaming Baby Express. For some reason, people with infants really like to take the first flight east on New Year's Eve, which was the same flight I caught at 5 am to meet up with the rest of the team by afternoon in Boston. From there we boarded a plane to Zurich.

Somewhere over the Atlantic, it had turned midnight, which the Swissair pilot announced loudly in perfect German, then English, then French. I looked up at Nellie with bleary, accusing eyes and she grinned back, then returned her attention to her *Cosmo* magazine. We had scored a center row of seats in the smoking section so that we could spread out for the journey. Rebecca was stuck in a middle seat between two very large snoring adults whose arms billowed over their armrests and into her space. Her seating was her own fault because she refused to sit in the smoking section. Greta was snoozing in a window seat.

"Look at that." I nodded my head towards Greta. "Not a care in the world."

"Oh, I don't know about that," Nellie said. "She's starting to get the squeeze just like we did."

"And still do," I corrected her. "You know Ken's just waiting for something better to come along."

"Probably. But he's good and stuck with us until then."

Greta was now traveling with the technical team. She hadn't cracked the top 40 in any of the December speed events. Plus, with Donna gone for the season and Natalie still recovering, they had to fill spots on the technical team roster.

Nellie looked over at her with a look that bordered on kindness. "I actually feel sorry for her."

"So she gets all the breaks and you feel sorry for her?"

"Yeah, kinda. I know it's weird, but in a way getting dumped so much has left me a lot more prepared than she is. When you think about it, she's never done anything but wait for a plane ticket to come in the mail, go where she's supposed to go and do as she's told. First it was her parents, then the academy, then the US Ski Team. She has no idea what to do when somebody isn't taking care of her. She's like an eternal puppy. I could have been just like her."

"You mean, until you got the privilege of being kicked outside and left for dead?"

"Well, at least I'm much better prepared for whatever happens. I have some life skills."

"Like making pizza?" I was referring to one of our low points, after our second knee injuries, when Ken wouldn't let us train with the team. Nellie and I had rented a room in Boulder and trained with the University of Colorado ski team. We had both gotten jobs at a pizzeria in Boulder so that we could at least eat well.

"I am quite sure Greta can't spin dough above her head." Nellie smiled. I was beginning to think that being in college, even for a few months, had revealed her hidden Buddhist side.

"You're a better person than me," I readily admitted. "She ticks me off."

"Oh, don't get me wrong," Nellie corrected. "I don't *like* her…but I do feel sorry for her."

We landed in the gray fog of a European winter. The Alps may be the home of Alpine skiing, but they are rarely blessed with good early season snow, and this year was no exception. The air was cold and damp when we piled into two separate vans and headed our separate ways. The technical skiers headed to some Europa Cups in France, while we speed skiers went to the first World Cup race of the new year, a Super G. It had been moved from a lower elevation resort to the highest non-glacier skiing available, the Arlberg Alps. The same weather pattern that caused the "inversion" that kept all the fog pressed into the chilly lowlands made it warm and sunny in the swishy resort of Lech, where our five-star hotel was within sight of the finish area. Wealthy, immaculately-dressed Europeans strolled the main street, ambling in and out of expensive boutiques. Anna would have loved it here.

During the short Christmas break, I had gotten to see Anna at Barton Memorial Hospital a few times. It had been nearly three years since my last stay, and I no longer knew every nurse by name. Anna's bed was decked out with Christmas lights and ornaments, and she even managed to have a clean bow in her hair. She insisted on watching the replay of her crash on TV, pausing it at the moment of impact.

"I'm coming back, Sharpie," she promised.

I couldn't look at the TV, so I looked at her. "I know you are. If anyone can do it, you can."

We had lost Anna and Greta but picked up Linda, who was more patched up than recovered, and Ella. Ella had never raced a World Cup in Europe. Being "fed to the wolves" as a rookie on the World Cup was definitely not ideal for her own skiing at this point (and further justified the Canadian's body bag comment), but her fresh attitude was good for the rest of us. Some of us, that is.

Lucy didn't like Ella much. Actually, she had hated her ever since this past fall in Europe when we had all gone shopping together. Lucy had a thing for shoplifting. It went back to her middle school days, where petty theft at the massive shopping mall in her hometown was not only a hobby but also a sort of initiation rite among bored preteens. It was part of the reason her parents had sunk all the resources from their carpeting business into her skiing. She didn't need to steal anymore now that she had all her expenses paid and was making big-time money. But she liked the thrill of it and loved showing off the prizes she had smuggled—clothing she had put on under her own in the dressing room, bracelets she tried on and never took off, even trinkets she never intended to use. It made the rest of us uncomfortable, but we never did anything about it. Ella was different. She walked right up to the shopkeeper in the first store we entered.

"Excuse me. Do you speak English?"

"Ein bischen...a leetle," the shopkeeper replied shyly.

"That girl right over there. See her?" Ella pointed straight to Lucy.

"Ja, ja. I do."

"She's going to try to steal something from you. *Stehlen*. Do you understand?"

"Ja, Verstehen!" The shopkeeper answered, fixing her eyes on Lucy who scowled at Ella then huffed out of the store, leaving us to shop in peace. The two had barely spoken since.

Any pressure we felt in December doubled down in January. This was it—the last month to qualify for the Olympics. The qualification criteria were tattooed on our brains: One top 5, two top 10s or three top 15s. They might fill out the team with whoever had the next best results, but what Nellie had said in Copper Mountain stuck in my mind. If you're not one of the best in the world, why bother going to the Olympics?

I had decided that under the circumstances, with all these injuries, it wasn't enough just to make the team. I wanted to qualify by the same standards as the great '84 team. Depending on how things went here, along with my top ten finish in Sestriere, I was either half or a third of the way there. With that in mind, I was disappointed to finish 16th in Lech. Even though it was a good race for me and the top American result, it didn't do me any good.

After the race was over, we ambled back to the hotel. We had no twisting drive through post-race traffic and crowds, no rush to pack up and move out. It was a sunny afternoon, and we had two more days to explore the Arlberg Alps on skis while staying in Lech at a gorgeous hotel with ridiculously fabulous gourmet food. Even though nobody was jubilant, the walk "home" felt luxurious. All of us except for Howard, who we assumed had found some old friends at the outdoor schnapps bar, reassembled in the hotel restaurant overlooking the river. We hadn't noticed that an hour after the race had ended, the finish area was still crowded. Waitresses delivered bowls of tomattencremesuppe while we helped ourselves to the salad bar.

We were just digging into our salads when Howard suddenly appeared in the doorway across the room. He hurried towards us, weaving his oversized body through tightly placed tables of quiet vacationers. When he was still a few tables away he could no longer contain himself.

"They're disqualifying the Austrians for safety pins!" Howard's outburst stopped us all short. Having our full attention, he quickly explained what he knew.

"The Swiss coach noticed that Anita Wachter had her bib tightened up with safety pins. The other coaches said they'd seen Brunni (the Austrian trainer) pinning all their bibs at the start. And alteration to a race bib is against FIS rules. So far just Wachter is out for sure, but they may take them all out."

Sepp had grabbed the radio slung on the back of his chair and was heading outside.

"Turn on your radio, Steve!" He was out the door. Howard paused, unsure of whether to fill us in at the table or head back to the finish area in search of more scoop. In a moment, he turned around and hustled to the door. "Wait up Sepp!"

In a few minutes, Sepp's voice came across the radio: "They're having it out pretty good right now, but it looks like Wachter and Eder are out for sure. Wolf is iffy." Sigrid Wolf had not only won the race but also had grown up one village down the road. Disqualifying the hometown girl in her home country was an ungracious thing to do to the town that had rallied to host the race at the last minute.

As I ate, I thought about what a bummer that would be for the Austrian girls. But then my mood perked up. If this decision held, I'd be one race closer to qualifying. By the time our salad plates were cleared, Sepp's voice came across the radio.

"It's official. Wolf, Wachter and Eder are all out." Then he added: "I think the Swiss team is packing up and getting out of here as soon as possible."

I couldn't help smiling. It reminded me of that commercial where the woman is relaxing while her oven cleaner is at work. Just while eating lunch I was moving up in the results: 16th, 15th, 14th, 13th…Thirteenth place and a new shot of hope.

After the race in Lech, and for the first time in nearly a year, we used our time on snow to relax. Things had changed since Anna's accident. Now it felt like the coaches were trying to protect us more than push us. They still probably hoped we would be the Bad News Bears of the ski world and surprise everyone but, with a month to go until the Olympics, they realized we needed help relieving the intensity, not adding to it. For two days, we meandered around the giant sun-drenched Arlberg Alps on skis, having lunch and stopping for cappuccinos at little mountain huts. Once again we felt like a team and we drove over the Arlberg Pass refreshed.

Our next stop was another high altitude Swiss resort, Zinal. A really good yodeler could stand high on the hill in Leukerbad and be heard directly across the Rhone Valley in Zinal. We made the sign of the cross, as if warding off evil spirits when we passed the turnoff to Leukerbad, then we veered toward the other side of the valley and up a steep road that Howard described best as being "so twisting it could unhitch a snake." At the top of the road sat the village of Zinal, above which the mountains opened into a giant treeless expanse. Our course descended spectacularly down a steep icy pitch, then hit a huge man-made jump and emptied into a long flat. Man-made jumps—created to generate an exciting hazard, or merely a visible spot for a sponsor's banner—are generally trouble. They don't match the terrain's natural flow and usually lack an appropriate landing zone. This one, featuring a sports drink banner, made us all a bit nervous.

"Thank God we're not in the first seed," Jenna whispered to me before the first training run. "I've got to check this out before I can run it."

The two of us found a spot above the start where we could see down the entire upper steep and the jump. The first two racers were Germans. Except for the Americans, every national team had a specific style: the Austrians stood up tall in slalom; the Swiss used a narrow stance and a lot of knee angulation; the Italians stayed in a very compact position; and the Yugoslavians rippled loosely down the hill like Slinkys. These styles developed over years of exposure to the same coaches and technical philosophies. Our national style, if we had one, was best described as scrappy because the only consistent factor in our coaching staff was its inconsistency. The Germans were known for their smooth and disciplined skiing, even on sheer ice, so we knew we would get a good visual image by watching them.

Jenna and I sat on a mound of snow as the first racer left the gate. Regina Mosenlechner carried good speed off the top section and diced the steep turns with German precision, carrying maximum speed towards the jump.

"Nice!" Just as I said it, she threw in a giant check turn, dumped her speed and still sailed off the jump, barely landing before the flats.

Next up was Mosenlechner's teammate, Michaela Gerg who had left the gate before the radios started buzzing. Gerg, too, skied the top beautifully, but she didn't do a check turn before the bump. We watched her go up and up and up, and finally drop out of sight on the other side of the bump. Instead of seeing her reappear, we saw an explosion of equipment—skis and poles erupting across the flats. This time every radio lit up with static and frantic calls: "Halt!", "Stop!", "%^#&!". The lucky third racer was flagged off the course before the jump. Within minutes the rest of us waiting to take our runs were putting our clothes back on. By the time we skied down the pitch a snow cat was busily churning the bump apart.

Once the bump had been significantly shaved, training resumed without incident. When we saw the first training run times, Steve was giddy. "Look at your split times. You were 4th on the flats!" This erased any doubt about my skis which gave Steve a jolt of confidence.

Racers weren't the only ones battling. The reps had their own races to win. Selling skis is big business in Europe, and ski racers are high profile, household names. All you had to do was look at any magazine rack to know that Maria Walliser skied on Volkl, Michaela Figini on Atomic, Erica Hess on Rossignol. Each rep wanted his skis to be the fastest and to win the downhill, the most visible event at the Olympics

Many factors, and a little magic, go into making a fast ski. Beyond the hours of base preparation and the perfect wax for that day's snow conditions, fast skis have just the right base material from the factory. Plastic base material comes off of giant spools like huge rolls of thick duct tape and gets pressed into the ski. Some sections within the spool, for reasons uncertain, are faster than others, but there is no way to know that until the skis are tested on snow. Once the reps figure out which skis are fast, they scramble back to the factory in search of more skis made from that same section of the spool and grab them for their racers. Steve had done well for me.

Of course, like highly charged racehorses, these babies were hard to control, and I clearly hadn't mastered them. But even after a ragged ride down the steeps, my runs were within striking distance of the leaders. More importantly, Steve and I knew we had a bit of magic on our side.

Steve was normally the mellowest person on the planet. He was enthusiastic when I did well and forgiving when I sucked. Therefore, I was surprised after our final training run to see him red-faced and agitated, pacing next to our row of skis by the chairlift.

"What's got your fur up?' I asked him jokingly, thinking it was an act.

"See that guy?" I followed his gaze to a rep from another company rapidly skiing away.

"He just tried to take your skis. Yesterday he was trying to take them apart to look at the bases, so I was watching him."

Even if he was just going to look at the bases, that's like stealing the other team's play book before the game. Very dirty pool. In a way, though, it was a real turning point. If we were worth messing with, we were getting somewhere.

"Cool!" I said, acknowledging the implication. Steve finally smiled.

On the first race day, Lucy, Rebecca and Jenna all finished in the top fifteen: "in the points." These were Jenna's and Rebecca's first World Cup points ever, and it was Lucy's best race all year. It was huge for the entire team's confidence and morale. If Jenna and Rebecca were officially no longer rookies, and Lucy was back on track and we had fast skis, maybe—just maybe—we could contend as a team. We weren't the Swiss, who were now in the habit not only of winning but also of sweeping the top 3 places, but we might have a chance as dark horses. The next day I charged out of the start, got tossed like a rag doll on the steeps and even heard Sepp yell, "Yeeeow!", as I bounced past him on my hip and recovered. I finished best of our team in 15th, and with that officially qualified for the Olympic team, the old fashioned way.

Our final stop was in Bad Gastein, Austria. This is where the Olympic Team would be named as soon as our downhills were over and the technical team rejoined us from their races in Slovenia. The word "bad" means bath in German. Like Leukerbad this place was named for its mineral baths. Also like Leukerbad, for us "bad" just meant bad sometimes. I'd heard this downhill was among the hairiest and, true to my inner chicken, I was really nervous the afternoon before our first training run. I told myself later that I must have needed to relieve my anxiety, and that's why I lapsed into some punk-like behavior.

Ella and I were walking around town and saw Lucy, all spiffed up in her white leather jacket, walking with one of the French coaches. The cutest one, of course. They were cradling steaming cups of sweet, spiced "gluhwein" they'd gotten from a street vendor, Lucy was laughing at everything he said. This was the side of Lucy the press saw.

"She must really be after him if she's blowing calories on *that* stuff." As I said it, Ella was already pulling a schladi from her pocket and giving me a devious look. We ducked into a narrow alley and waited until they'd passed. Ella lit the Schladi and lobbed it underhanded so that it rolled past their feet, and we sprinted down the alley as fast as we could. We didn't stop when we heard the bang. We made sure to take a long detour back to the hotel so that it looked like we'd come from the other direction. When we came into the hotel, the man at the front desk was talking to a maid in German, giving some sort of instructions as they both inspected a white leather jacket, spattered with burgundy streaks. A vision of Lucy, dripping in sticky wine, like the pigs-blood-meets-prom-queen scene from the movie *Carrie*, sprung to my mind. Ella and I caught each other's eyes, registered twin "Oh Scheisse!" looks and hurried to our rooms. At least Lucy would never be able to trace it to us.

As in Lech, the Bad Gastein hotel was far too fancy for the likes of us. It felt more like a palace with marble staircases and a formal dining room with high ceilings, white linens and brightly polished silver. I doubted they'd had many guests who jumped rope in the halls and did sets of sprints up the steps. And, they certainly weren't accustomed to guests who tested the acoustics like we did when Lucy followed me out of the breakfast room the next day. I soon discovered that voices resonate alarmingly well in a wide marble stairwell. Lucy's stress meter was already bent, but our "joke," had pushed it off the charts. Even in the best of times, there had always been tension between us like we were in a subtle tug-of-war. It was no big deal when she was beating me but, ever since I had become her "equal" on the hill, the tension had been building. In that instant, something snapped.

"You threw that schladi, didn't you?"

I didn't answer. Technically I hadn't actually thrown it.

"All you think about is yourself," she continued.

I knew we'd gone over the edge with the schladi, and I hadn't thought of how it would affect someone who was already balancing on a thin edge. I felt bad for that and I was on the verge of making a private vow to make it up to Lucy in kindness. Maybe I'd listen to some stories about her boyfriend or ask for diet advice. But then she pushed the one big red button she shouldn't have pushed.

"You think you're so much better than the rest of us!" She hurled it out like some final, damning accusation. I was speechless, partially because a gray-haired, well-dressed spa couple who hadn't had their coffee yet were looking at us like we were insane and partly because I was so thoroughly appalled. If anyone thought she was better than the rest, it was Lucy with her big contracts, fancy agent and perpetual supply of boyfriends. And regardless of all that, didn't each of us believe we could be the very best and wasn't that the point of being here in the first place? Hadn't I finally earned the right to feel like I belonged among the best? Ever since I was 14, I'd let myself believe the US Ski Team coaches who had said I wasn't good enough, that I was too smart, or too fat, or too old, or too slow in the stupid 12-minute run. Meanwhile the Lucy's of the world just plugged ahead no matter what anyone said, demanded the attention they needed and used it to fuel their momentum. Now, finally, I had confidence, finally believed in myself enough to take off. And I was getting slammed for it?

Anger boiled up in me, not just towards Lucy but towards everyone who'd had a part in undermining my path. How dare she! How dare they! That's what I was *thinking*. But what came out of my mouth was something like a cough or a hairball that got stuck in my throat. I stormed past Lucy and out of the stairwell, slamming the door so hard behind me that hallway chandelier quivered, and a surprised maid scurried from my path.

Things on the hill were equally grim. Winter had finally arrived, sort of, and the weather was horrendous. We honed our hurry-up-and-wait skills killing time in the damp lodge that smelled like roasted onions, cigarettes and body odor, waiting for the fog to clear or the wind to abate or the rain to let up slightly. Whenever it did, we would rush en masse to the start for a training run, which was usually interrupted by crashes and course holds. At least the course wasn't so bad. The only big air on the course was one huge bump we could see from the start. On the last training run, we watched the Russian girl, who ran right before Rebecca, go off it. One arm and one ski tip flew up before she was sucked over and out of sight.

Rebecca had never fully recovered from watching Anna's crash on TV. She hadn't admitted it, but I could see it in her skiing. She was skiing fine on sunny days when conditions were just right, like in Zinal. But on ugly days or when her confidence dipped for whatever reason she held back, like she didn't really want to be there. It was that kind of defensive skiing that had cost her a spot in the World Championships downhill, and I knew she didn't want to make that mistake again. In the starting gate that day, her eyes told the truth. They made me think of the promise I'd made my grandmother: not to do anything I didn't want to do. Suddenly, I wondered if anyone had ever told *her* she was precious. But it was too late to tell her now.

No flag went up to stop the race after the Russian, so Rebecca started. As soon as she went over the bump, the radios erupted. The Russian hadn't made it and, in fact, was being tended to by a ski patrol whose toboggan was exactly where Rebecca landed a moment later. As if hit by a sniper, another one bit the dust. That night I visited Rebecca in her room. Seeing her with her bandaged leg propped up, her arm in a cast and a puffy bloody lip, I saw pain and also, for the first time ever, relief in her eyes. She had been struggling. She might have made the Olympic team, might have finally proved she could earn her spot rightfully, but now there was no question. No more grinding away, no more stress. It was over.

We got word from the men's team about their results from the final training run in Kitzbuhel. Eric had achieved his goal and earned a spot to race the Hahnenkamm. On race day, in an effort to maximize his speed, he tucked straight off the first jump, the "Mausefalle" or mousetrap. He ended up launching over the safety fencing, and sustaining a pretty serious head injury among other things. He was out for at least a month if not the rest of the season. I thought about how much downhill meant to Eric and about the body bag comment made by the Canadian. He *was* too young to run Kitzbuhel, just like Nellie had come back from her injuries too soon and Anna was trying too hard to prove the coaches wrong. Perhaps nobody could have saved them from themselves, held them back at the bit for their own good, but I wished somebody had tried.

As the night of the final Olympic team selection approached, the tension reached an all time high. Lucy and I weren't speaking, everyone was sad about Rebecca and, barring any miraculous performances, everyone in our hotel pretty much knew who would make the Olympic team in the speed events. Dan decided it was the perfect time for the ABC crew that had been following us around to do a group interview and show what great teammates and friends we were.

Before the interview started, they told us they needed certain shots and made us look at each other in turn for ten seconds. Then we did it again, looking as if we were listening to that person speak...and again looking serious and again laughing. The whole thing was a set-up by Dan. He had consulted with the producer, who knew from experience that if two people maintain eye contact long enough, they connect in some way. After the shots, we answered questions:

"How do you balance being close teammates and fierce competitors?... How do you maintain mutual respect and support amidst pre-Olympic stress?..."

Partway through, we figured out we'd been somewhat tricked, but we bought into it. After all we *wanted* to behave decently and have compassion for each other's efforts. And besides, we had no choice. Being on a team means you're all in it together. In tearing down each other, you eventually tear down yourself.

The technical team selection came down to one final time trial between Greta and Nellie. Neither had scored a World Cup point this season though Nellie had some top 10 individual runs. She just hadn't put two of them together. They had two runs each of GS and Slalom.

Nellie won three of them.

The night of the team selection was far more emotionally charged than any of us had imagined it would be. We gathered in the hotel's lounge, and Ken read the list of nine women. Only two members on the list had been to an Olympics. When he announced the last spot, I honestly thought he was joking. But then I looked around and noticed Nellie was missing. Tears sprang to my eyes and I couldn't get myself to look at Greta.

When Ken was finished congratulating Greta, he turned towards me. I intercepted his look with as blank a stare as I could manage and shook my head ever so slightly. He stepped towards me and put out his hand. There was no use making a scene, so I shook his hand and accepted his congratulation. When I let go of his hand, he kept mine for a moment and leaned towards me.

"It was her choice," he said in a low voice before releasing my hand and turning away.

As quickly as I could without raising attention, I wove through the crowded lobby and made my way to the staircase, bounding up the marble steps to the fourth floor and Nellie's room. I knocked on the door. No answer. I knocked again, harder.

"Come in!" came a voice from inside.

Nellie was sitting on her bed, legs outstretched and her back against the wall. She had her Walkman cranked and was reading *Sports Illustrated*. She looked up at me, smiling, and took off her headphones.

"Congratulations!" She said it calmly, sincerely. I didn't smile or say thank you or make any pretense of the pleasantry that filled the lobby. Instead I pushed to the point.

"What happened?"

"What do you mean?"

"Why weren't you with us?"

"Oh. Well, I knew I didn't make it, so I asked Ken if I could sit this one out." Apologetically, she added, "I know I should have been there for the team, but...well, enough's enough, you know?" Her voice just barely wavered on the last part.

"I *mean*, why weren't you on the team. You made it fair and square. You beat Greta in the time trials. You earned your spot."

It wasn't until Nellie's expression relaxed that I knew how hard she was trying to hold it together. Her smile faded and her voice softened.

"Olivia. I did it again. I tweaked my knee in the last time trial. She deserves to go."

"And you don't?! You've won Europa Cups, you've scored in World Cups. You can ski slalom on one leg better than that little...ugh!"

"I'm better than her when I'm at my best, but I'm not at my best. I haven't been at my best in three years. Every time I get close, I get hurt again."

"So race in the Olympics and then back off. Afterwards you can take all the time you need to get better."

Nellie sighed. "I've tried that. It never works. I'm tired of fighting all the time. Greta's good and she's young and she's heading in the right direction. She deserves the chance."

This could not be happening. How could someone work so hard, endure so much, and just give it away?

"What about Australia?" I asked in one last ditch effort. She just shook her head.

"You know how I feel about that. To go, just for the sake of saying I was in the Olympics...I couldn't do that."

It was no use trying to change her mind, so we just sat there in a heavy, hopeless silence.

"Well, at least you're consistent," I managed to say after a few moments of mulling.

"Meaning what?"

"You always do the right thing. Like that time when we stole the ice cream from the Dragon Lady at that hotel in Austria. Ken looked like he really might kill us, and you were the only one to confess."

"How do you know I was being good? Maybe I *wanted* to be on the 'next plane home.' If only Ken had meant it, I could have missed the rest of that lousy trip."

For the first time we both laughed, remembering the good old bad days. But I couldn't let go of what bugged me most.

"It just seems...I mean, good guys are supposed to win. It just doesn't seem fair."

"What's that you always say? Gravity is fair? I guess it's true."

"I don't say that, do I?" Nellie looked a little flustered for a moment but brushed it off.

"Well, whatever; somebody does." Before I could say anything more, she shooed me out of her room. "Now get out of here and call your parents or do something constructive like light a schladi under Ken's window."

She grabbed her magazine and put her Walkman back on, and I left her alone.

I totally respected and understood Nellie's reasoning, but I doubted I would ever have the courage to do what she had done. That, I thought to myself, is the mark of a real champion.

Chapter 16:
Crash Course in Survival

There was one last stop for the entire team, the US Nationals in Colorado. Nellie headed straight back to Boulder. This time she wasn't in any rush to have surgery. CU's ski coach had suggested she try out for their cycling team. Cycling requires extreme hard headedness (something she had) and does not require fully intact ACLs'(something it appeared she might never have). If she made the cycling team, she could slip right into their spring training season. She already had it worked out by the time we boarded our plane in Zurich.

"I'll come watch you guys in the Nationals though. I promise."

"C'mon, Nellie. Won't that be torture?"

In the past two days, I had seen how hard it was for any of the girls who hadn't made the Olympic team to be around those of us who had. We wanted desperately to get to the Olympics, and they wanted just as desperately to get away from all talk of the Olympics.

"It'll be fine. Plus, I promised Blake I'd be there." She smiled at me as it finally registered.

"You and Blake…"

"Yep."

"Since when?"

"He took me to the ski ball in Denver."

"So, when I saw him that morning in Saas Fee…"

"It wasn't what you thought. We were just talking in my room, and we didn't know how late it was. When he figured out he'd missed the last train, he stayed on the couch. We both still felt weird about it though. I mean, I know how much you liked him, so at first it didn't seem right. I was wondering when you'd figure it out."

"Keine ahnung," I said, still somewhat dazed. I'd had no clue at all.

"He told me about how Lucy tried to attack him in Val D'Isere. I wish I could have seen that."

"Yeah, it wasn't pretty." I laughed remembering that scene, and my mind put together all the missing pieces that now added up. "So, if he was in Saas Fee…Greta knew?"

"Even Greta."

"Wow. Where was I?" I asked it to myself, but out loud, while wondering what else I had missed.

"You've been pretty focused."

"Looking out for number one," I said, thinking back to my conversation in Saas Fee with Dan, and not liking at all how that phrase sounded when it was about me.

"You make it sound like a bad thing, not noticing that one of your best friends was going out with the love of your life. Do you know how many people would die for that kind of tunnel vision?"

She had a point, but something still bugged me.

"But Lucy was right," I said, reliving the scene in the stairwell.

"Yeah, she was right. But she's a hypocrite to make you feel bad about it because it's worked pretty well for her. The only way you made it through was by believing in yourself when nobody else did. Don't apologize for that."

Crested Butte, CO:

"It looks like Vietnam down here! There are skis and poles everywhere. People are flying off the jump and exploding all over the place."

Unlike the other coaches, who had sugarcoated their course reports, downplaying how much faster the course was running on race day, Sepp gave me the unsweetened truth. His position atop the CYS (short for check your shorts) bump on the National Championships downhill course gave him a perfect view of the hollow where you would land if you screwed up the takeoff or "missed your move." A "move" is what you do to absorb the bump and minimize airtime. Pull your feet up too early or too late—miss your move—and you take off like an airplane, also referred to as "pulling a Lufthansa."

"Use your head today. No Lufthansa's, uh?" Sepp advised.

Two days earlier I had knocked out my front tooth slalom training and made a trip to Boulder for an emergency root canal. There was no reason for me to train slalom other than to get ready for the Combined event, an event which meant nothing to me. Ken had convinced me it made sense to prepare for the Combined in the Olympics because it would be one more medal chance. I thought about Donna's first win, which had been in a Combined, and despite Dan's warning about spreading myself too thin, I had jumped at the chance. Now it felt like I was caught in some twisted video game where hazards kept popping up the closer I got to my goal.

I really wanted to take Sepp's advice, to use my head and play it safe but, when it comes to rational thought you can't trust an athlete. The moment I got in the starting gate, the competitive part of my brain kidnapped the rational part of my brain and unlocked that extra gear I hadn't yet found in downhill. I nailed the top turns and headed down the "waterfall," an accelerator chute. It felt faster than in training. (Later I learned I was going 78 mph—not shabby for an "easy" downhill.) "Here comes the bump," I thought. "Ok, it is definitely faster." By the time I could adjust, I had missed my move by a mile and was sailing over Vietnam, headed for a hard landing smack in the hollow.

Falling on the steeps, with the combined effects of gravity and velocity, is spectacular. But falling on the flats is deadly. The impact of going from 80 to zero in an instant rarely turns out well. In the air prior to impact, I was amazed by how much time I had to think. I wondered what Sepp was thinking as he watched; what would hit first; how I would be hurt; what I would say to my parents on the phone; what the extent of my injuries would be; whether or not I would come back from this one; and, most acutely, how it would feel to watch the Olympics on TV—again.

I hit, hard, but my bindings popped off on impact, and I managed to tumble a bit instead of sticking firmly in the ground and having body parts break. I hurt, but in a general way and not excruciatingly in any one place. I got up. I shook off. I had never been so happy after a crash. With a sore body, a fat lip and a big smile on my face, I was going to the Olympics.

Chapter 17:
Five Ring Circus

"Welcome to CalGARY!"

A congregation of smiling people in red and white coats and big white cowboy hats greeted us as we got to baggage claim. The flight from Denver was short anyway, but on this day it felt like it only took about ten minutes. The Olympics had been an exciting concept, a fantasyland that existed somewhere beyond reality. Now that we were in Calgary, the fantasy rose up in full color, like the Magic Kingdom and welcomed us inside.

Our first stop was an airport hotel where we went through Olympic "processing." This was quite different from the processing we saw at the bologna plant on the Turkey Tour. First we were drug and gender tested (in case anyone had changed drastically from the year before), and then we were issued our official credentials that we were instructed by many officials to wear at all times. They wouldn't tell us what would happen if we lost them, but I suspect it would have involved an embassy and DNA testing.

Then the fun started. Volunteers guided us through a

series of rooms where we tried on each piece of our opening ceremonies outfits, followed by the red, white and blue medals ceremony uniform we all hoped to need. After those outfits came jean jackets and leather jackets, and an assortment of casual wear, workout wear, luggage, rings, watches, cameras, hats and official this's and thats. Our regular sponsors had also given us new Olympic competition uniforms before we left Colorado, so it felt like about ten Christmases. Camera crews followed us throughout the entire process, capturing the sight of kids in the ultimate candy store, and interviewed us at random to peek inside our bags and show off our swag. At one point, Jenna stepped back to look at her two bulging duffel bags, brand new right to the name tags.

"We might as well have shown up naked!"

After packing our haul into the vans, we went directly to the Olympic Village and checked in through tight security and metal detectors. We passed game rooms and TV rooms, a disco, a movie theater, a 24-hour cafeteria and even a McDonalds. At computer kiosks throughout the village we could punch in the ID number from our credential and send anyone else with a credential an electronic message. So, if a Russian Nordic skier thought a Japanese ice skater was cute, he could simply send her a message. The possibilities (and the potential complications) of that new technology seemed endless. Everything in the village was free and athletes dressed in team sweat suits were happily hunkered in, making themselves at home.

Already there was buzz surrounding some of the athletes. There were the bobsledders—the unlikely Jamaican bobsled team as well as Chicago Bears wide receiver Willie Gault who was on the US bobsled team.

And the much-hyped skaters like Katarina Witt and Debbie Thomas who looked like cake-top dolls in real life. Whenever we walked through the village, we saw athletes posing with each other for pictures to show back home. We dropped our things in a cluster of rooms designated for our team. Nakiska, where the Alpine races would be held, was more than an hour's drive north, and we would stay there during our competitions, cycling back to the village in between.

The men were already at Nakiska because the men's downhill competition kicked off the Games the following day. Ken hadn't wanted them to attend the Opening Ceremonies because they were "too much of a distraction," but the boys sent an electronic message to the organizing committee and made their own arrangements. After their final training run an official Olympic vehicle picked them up and sped them straight to the village with a police escort. By the time Ken, back in Nakiska, noticed they were missing, the boys were already halfway to Calgary. They arrived just as we were suiting up for the Opening Ceremonies.

We pulled on our wool skirts, sweaters and shearling boots, then topped that off with scarves, fedora hats and long white coats. We were sweltering by the time we arrived outside the stadium where all 1,122 men and 301 women from 57 nations milled around, waiting until it was time to march. In the raw, windy parking lot, I was grateful for our layers and hoped my family was warm in their seats. My entire family, though I hadn't yet seen them, were there to share the experience they had helped create.

From the sounds of the crowd, it must have been a pretty good show inside, especially when the Air Force jets ripped across the sky. Finally, we were corralled into line country by country and slowly moved towards the stadium, then into the dark concrete passage underneath it. In the seconds before we emerged, all the years of steady work and unsteady progress seemed to converge, racing towards one radiant moment of recognition.

My mind suddenly hit a rewind button and played back images of the opening ceremonies I'd watched stretched out on my belly in pajamas in front of the TV: Innsbruck in 1976, I remembered seeing the athletes march into view, little specks waving their flags to the world; in 1980 I spotted our hometown girl Natalie Scott in the Lake Placid parade; and then the hazy morphine-induced visions of Sarajevo from my hospital bed in 1984. This time I was on the other side of the screen and it felt completely unreal. We emerged from the tunnel into sudden, all-encompassing brightness, and reality burst open like a giant firework against the sky. Between the roar of the cheering crowd and my own heart, I barely heard the announcer boom:

"Etats Unis! The United States of America!"

Thousands of cameras flashed, turning the stands into a sparkling sea. We waved our flags and beamed supersized smiles, the kind that start inside and push all the way out to your ears. Everyone had a story about what it took to get here, a story made more real by all those who weren't here. I thought about Anna, Rebecca, Donna and Nellie, about Jamie and Luke and the mountain of friends and teammates who hadn't made it here and who were watching, or not, from somewhere else. I realized that for the past seven years, ever since I admitted that this is what I wanted most, I hadn't let myself imagine that this moment might really happen. If I had let myself see this last bit and had it snatched away, like so many little hopes along the way...well, none of that mattered anymore. As our mass of athletes oozed forward, looking up and around in every direction and waving, another American athlete bumped into me.

"Whoever said getting there is half the fun hasn't been here," he shouted. "This is amazing!"

Once we got situated in the stands, we got to enjoy the rest of the show and bask in the satisfaction of being Olympians. On this day we were all equal. Tomorrow there would be medalists and heroes, dissolved dreams and heads hung in disappointment. But today we shared the same victory.

After the ceremonies, we headed back to the Olympic Village for a Bryan Adams concert. There, even more so than at the Opening Ceremonies, the notion of all of us athletes being one big Olympic family really sunk in. It wasn't just the foreign athletes and non-skiers that were new to me before this day. I didn't even know a single Nordic or Jumping athlete ("Nordie") on our own US Ski Team. Their anonymity from the public awareness made us Alpine skiers ("Pineys") seem like rock stars by comparison, something that seemed especially unjust considering the sheer physical torture of training and competing in the Nordic events. But here any distinctions based on media popularity didn't exist. On this dance floor, filled with the world's best athletes, the American ski jumper who casually worked a standing back flip into his dancing, was the star of the show, earning a chorus of multilingual cheers.

Our "Piney" boys knew they should drive straight back north to Nakiska but, instead, they decided to stay with us in the village. Not because they liked us so much but because they wanted to get a good night's sleep.

"What's wrong with our hotel up there?" I asked innocently.

The guys shared a knowing look with each other.

"It's just a little loud," said one.

"And small," said another.

Now they exchanged mischievous looks.

"But it has a great view."

"And it's really outdoorsy."

They all looked at each other, their eyes glinting a shared secret.

Ken had told us we had comfortable accommodations close to the area. Having been to Nakiska the year before, I knew there wasn't much up there. The ski area was built expressly for the Olympics in the middle of a national park, so when I heard we were staying in a park it made sense. I had never been to the grand Canadian Pacific hotels in Banff and Lake Louise, but I'd seen pictures of them. I imagined this hotel would be a bit more rustic but still cool.

The next morning, we drove straight to the ski area to watch the men's race which was postponed for a day because a warm Chinook wind had blown in during the night, making the course a soupy mess. We free-skied a few runs by Braille in the fog, then decided to move into our rooms. Driving away from the ski area, we passed the only slopeside hotel. The Swiss had paid extra to make sure it was finished on time to accommodate their army of athletes, coaches, trainers, chefs and even hair stylists. Other than that, there were a few houses and condos sprinkled around a golf course and clubhouse. A sign on the clubhouse read "Kananaskis Country Club." Country Club seemed like a stretch, but it must be beautiful in the summer. We turned right, away from the road to Calgary, and civilization. Within a few minutes, we turned right again into a network of smaller roads that split off to individual parking pads. On those pads stood our hotels.

Suddenly I remembered the guys referring to each other as "trailer park trash," and it all made sense. That is, their *comments* made sense. Staying in a trailer park for the biggest event of our careers in the middle of winter made no sense at all.

"I thought the guys were kidding!" Jenna jumped out of the car first and started laughing. In her best Canadian accent, she turned back to us and pretended to be our host.

"Howdy folks, and welcome to the official Olympic trailer park, eh? Do you want a full or partial hook-up, eh?"

We slowly got out of the van to look at our new homes while a man in a thick parka who looked a lot like whoever Jenna was trying to imitate approached us. He smiled and handed Sepp a few sets of keys and pointed out four RVs. "Two to a vehicle is about right," he instructed. He opened one up and showed us how to operate the generator and the heater.

"Showers and toilets are over there. Hot showers are free, eh?" He smiled and pointed through the trees to a low concrete building about 200 yards away. "You can buy firewood for the pits at the check-in building. Your boys have been having some nice bonfires to take off the chill. You may not need that with the Chinook blowing through though. It's warmed right up, eh?"

With that he left us to try to cram our things into every available crevice of the RV's. Jenna and I were sharing one trailer, and she was already unpacking.

"I like it. Nobody will find us here."

"Yeah, except the bears." I imagined trudging through the snow in my jammies with wet hair after a free outdoor shower. I'd probably make a tasty bear treat. I looked again at the distant bathrooms and reminded myself not to drink any water at dinner.

Considering our situation, everyone stayed in remarkably good spirits. We were still high on the Olympic excitement, and Jenna did have a point. Apparently the ABC crew had already come to the park and filmed this scene, so no more reporters or cameras would bug us here. And we wouldn't have to run our friends and family through security if they wanted to visit to roast marshmallows or something, which was the only hospitality we could offer because we didn't really have room inside to entertain visitors.

That night, while we tried to sleep amidst the howling wind and the hum of generators, millions of people (with TVs that is) were tuning in to ABC. They saw the Swiss ski team dining at tables set with silver and white linen, then they were flashed to the American downhillers standing around a bonfire roasting hot dogs on the end of long sticks. The very next morning, as we were heading to the ski area for our first day of downhill training, Ken arrived at the park. We hadn't seen him since he arrived because he had been dealing with the Trustees and VIPs, for whom the team had somehow managed to find lodging close to the area. He had even missed the Opening Ceremonies, thinking he would set an example for the men's team, who missed seeing his example because they'd ditched him. He looked stressed out and disheveled, like he could use a free shower and some quality rest in the Winnebago.

"OK girls," he announced, in a flat voice. "Some rooms opened up at the Country Club. If anyone's interested, we can move your clothes over there after skiing today." Everyone except Jenna—who preferred the trailer park isolation—was so excited at the prospect of heating and indoor plumbing that we didn't ask how the rooms had materialized. The next morning, I picked up my skis in the ski room which was an entire huge parking garage under the lodge, where the reps tuned all their athletes' equipment. Steve could not wait to give me the scoop he had overheard the night before. Everything comes out in the ski room anyway, but especially when the reps from all the countries share the same giant ski room, with free beer.

"The second that ABC piece ran, the sponsors went nuts," he explained. Understandably, the sponsors wanted to know why, after giving so much money to the team for the "finest" training, our country's best athletes were staying in a trailer park. "And Shaklee?" Steve continued, "I heard they threatened to pull all their funding."

Shaklee very generously funded our entire sports medicine program. I cringed thinking of how the nutrition company must now feel about their sponsorship.

"Yeah, I can see that. I doubt they want to be associated with team weenie roast."

"It's not all bad, though," Steve added. "Apparently the Trustees were so embarrassed that some of them gave up their rooms for the athletes." That explained the sudden availability.

Once we got on the hill, surrounded by the same faces we'd see at any World Cup, everything began to feel normal. There were a few differences, like the army of cheerful course workers who spoke our language (kindly even) at every turn, and the herd of local bighorn sheep we had to pick our way through to get to the start area. You didn't see either of those things in Europe. We slipped into our normal routine on hill, inspecting the downhill as a group the first time.

The course plunged down two upper pitches, separated by a blind whoop-dee-doo knoll, then exited to the right around a huge tuna turn, after which you caught some air over another knoll by the Super G start, landed and immediately banked a left turn down a third steep pitch. One big jump launched you down a steep runway and into a big right turn that poured onto a long flat. Fast skis would be critical here. A final jump led into the giant finish stadium surrounded by scoreboards and bleachers aimed at the Jumbotron. It looked a bit like Zinal. If I could stay on my feet and out of the nets on top, I'd be fine.

After each training run, reporters swarmed us, thrusting out their tape recorders and asking questions, some about the course, but most about our predictions:

"Who do you think is the favorite?" "How will the Americans do?" and of course their favorite, "What are your chances for a medal?"

Jan, when she was at the end of her patience, which had been often by the time I got to know her, shot back a quite excellent response to such questions: "That's why they run the race!"

I tried to give a more positive spin but still keep it real: "Super G is really my strongest event, but my downhill is coming along. I just want to do my best on race day." Of course, those vanilla answers were not the chest-thumping sound bites they wanted.

They liked Lucy's comments better: "I've been

building up to this my whole life but especially for the past two years. I'm as ready as I'll ever be to go for the gold!"

And they really liked Ken's smug quotes: "Remember: Linda and Will were dark horses in 1984. Never count the Americans out. We're a breed apart." That last part was a tagline the marketing department had come up with just before the Games. He liked the way it sounded.

Ken was still selling the dream with slogans. Linda and Will, though unheralded, were hardly inexperienced when they won their medals in 1984. And the team hadn't exactly helped them capitalize on their success. Four years later, Will didn't even qualify for the Calgary Olympic Team, and Linda clearly had one ski boot out the door, totally burned out at 24. Neither of them lived the cereal box fairy tale that I had imagined a gold medal promised. As for the rest of us, our medal hopes were mostly hopes. Olympic medals are a miraculous confluence of talent, hard work, timing, experience and luck. We held our own on the first two, but the rest was iffy.

I didn't mind the press hype. It added to the energy of the event. The atmosphere was continually charged from the combined energy and enthusiasm of competitors, workers and spectators. It felt like a dream to be with my World Cup family yet be able to sit in the lodge and have lunch with my real family after each training run. The day before the downhill, I came into the lodge and saw Luke standing with my parents.

"I knew you'd make the team. I got my plane ticket two months ago." He wrapped me in a bear hug and we all got some lunch at the cafeteria. Eventually the talk turned to medals, like it always did.

"It's all about trajectory," Luke said, smiling at my

Dad.

"How about English?" I pretended to complain. Now that he was in graduate school in engineering, Luke and my dad really lost me in their conversations.

"The Olympics. They're all about trajectory. You're on an upward trend. It's more about where you're headed than where you are."

"So you're saying a medal is right in my path and I just have to intercept it?"

"Well, inertia and momentum help, too. But my point is you're definitely headed in the right direction." Luke wasn't nearly so bitter about ski racing anymore. In fact, he looked genuinely excited to watch the competition and he was definitely having a good time. Before I could ask about Molly, he told me that they'd broken up. "I *like* my ratty t-shirts," he explained, and I couldn't help smiling.

Everything made me smile. Even the security guards were cheerful, politely redirecting the fan who tried to roast a marshmallow over Nakiska's Olympic flame. I'd never seen so many fans, and they were going to cheer hard—for the medal winners and for the Lebanese racer who might finish five minutes behind the winner.

It certainly helped that the press expected nothing out of me. Unlike Natalie, our most successful skier ever, Linda, a reigning Olympic champion, and Lucy, our great hope in Downhill and Combined, I could compete without the fear of letting down my entire country. Besides, I knew the only way I'd pull off a medal miracle was to relax and think of anything but gold medals. Stressing out is way overrated.

Lucy had taken the opposite approach. This was to be *her* Olympics. Never mind that her trajectory had been heading the wrong direction most of the year, that her training run times had been slow and that her sawdust diet wasn't going to help her much on a course that favored someone built like a Mack truck. Never mind all signs to the contrary, not to mention the role sheer luck plays in ski racing—she was going to win a medal, dammit! As unlikely as that seemed, I had to admit that if anyone could pull off such a dramatic turnaround it would be Lucy.

The downhill race day arrived on a gray howling wind. Lucy had drawn number 3, not the ideal number for a course with a long flat section that would surely speed up as more racers skied the track. Her start number was the first thing to set her into a spin.

"Stay away from the lawnmower blade," Steve warned as I came through the ski room that morning. I could hear the stress in Lucy's voice as she fired questions at Drew.

"Who grabbed my poles?...Where are my extra goggles?...What did Sean do with the bag for extra clothes?!"

She was like the Tasmanian Devil cartoon character, spinning so fast it seemed she might vaporize. She probably needed a hug, but I certainly wasn't going to risk it. Instead I took Steve's advice and kept a safe distance. Usually that sort of meltdown improved by getting outside, but this time it got worse.

"Where are the coaches? What's with the training course? Who set this?"

Nothing was right, and I could see it in her eyes. They were wild and unfocused, making her look like a cornered animal as she approached the starting gate. She pushed out of the start, skittered around the three steep turns, then caught an edge right before the tuna turn, performing a spectacular eggbeater into the net. The tuna lay still on the ground.

Dan was on the scene in moments and, because his mind could not comprehend yet another disaster, he tried to stand Lucy up. She collapsed immediately, clutching her stomach as she coughed up a thin ribbon of blood. A team of ski patrol swarmed to her aid and carefully loaded her onto a backboard so that she could be airlifted to Calgary by helicopter. Meanwhile, back at the start, the delay ratcheted up the tension another few notches. It made great TV.

Once they were done with Lucy's dramatic evacuation, the press returned to the big story: which Swiss would win? Would it be Maria Walliser or Michaela Figini?

Cameras had shadowed each racer from her morning muesli to the starting gate. But Mother Nature was rooting for a German that day. Marina Kiehl won by a full second, and the Swiss blamed it all on a strong tailwind. Golnur Postnikova, the Russian who had won the final training run, missed a gate, the same gate Jenna missed. Both of them were only racing in this one event, and both were exceptionally bummed, but there was one huge difference. Jenna only had to go back to the trailer park. We never saw Postnikova again.

I finished best for the Americans in 18th. Not great but not horrible. I was too focused on the Super G to be disappointed. I knew I was a long shot but, like Luke had pointed out, with the right trajectory a medal was within reach.

At the hospital, doctors diagnosed Lucy with a mild concussion, whiplash and a bruised kidney. She also had bitten her lip which explained the blood. She was out for the Games, competition-wise. Appearance-wise, she was just getting started.

From her hospital bed she managed to give a TV interview. Someone had neatly woven her hair into two thick braids tied with red white and blue ribbons. I could practically hear her agent orchestrating just the right look to maximize the situation: "Pixies! America loves pixies!" So there she was, looking young and innocent and, in a brief unguarded moment, vulnerable. But the instant the interview started her smile returned, brighter than ever. A *Surge* bar, logo visible, rested on her bedside tray.

"I just want to get back to the mountain so I can watch my team," she sniffed to one reporter, pushing a stray lock of hair off her face with one hand, and using the other to gently nudge her boyfriend—who had flown from Florida to see her—out of the camera's shot.

"She'd never have gotten this much press if she'd raced," Drew told me when I had seen him in the ski room earlier. He was whistling as he strapped up a pair of skis for Lucy to hold during interviews if she did make it back to watch the races. "This injury is as good as gold!"

It wasn't a very sporting perspective, but he was right. After seeing Lucy in action all these years, I found it odd to see *her* being used so blatantly. She appeared to be enjoying the attention, but by now I knew her well enough to see it was an act. Maybe her hardest one.

This was it, my main event, and I felt good. Calm but excited. I felt strong on the warm-up course, dropping low in my tuck, running a clean ski and clipping each gate with just enough force to know I was on a fast line. After inspection I even had a few minutes to chill out with my family near the bottom of the chairlift. Dad kept his last words unusually brief. The moment felt so big, so heavy, and he probably didn't want to say the wrong thing.

"Good luck little person. I always knew you could do it."

"Aren't you going to ask me about my M.A., Dad?" I had to throw him a bone.

"Well, if you insist."

"It's W.A." He relaxed into an easy, satisfied smile, and gave me a hug.

"Have fun honey!" said my Mom. Her eyes were welling up.

My sisters kept it light, pretending to interview each other, "Well Bob, what do you think Olivia's chances are?" Laura asked, and Eliza responded, "They're pretty good, and we all know she's the prettiest one out there."

"And I'm precious!" I reminded them sternly. We all laughed.

Jamie was excited and nervous for me, and a little jealous. Maybe a lot jealous. This was his dream, too. I saw all those emotions in his face and heard them in his voice.

"Well O, this is it. I guess you know better than me what to do, so there's not much I can tell you now. But, well, hammer down!"

Then I saw Anna. She had made the trek to see us. A boy on the Canadian team may have had something to do with it, too. But she was there with a flag tucked in her jacket and ice picks on her crutches. It must have been torture for her to watch, but she did it with a smile and even took the time to pump me up before I got on the chairlift.

"Well, here goes nuthin'!"

"You made it! You've already shown everyone you can do it. Now ski your own race." She punched me in the arm, hard, a little good luck ritual she always did. Then she crutched back over to her spot amidst a jovial group of strapping guys with red maple leaves painted on their faces.

"Break a leg!" she called back. "I mean, not *really*."

I wore bib #7. It was my first time starting in the first seed, so I was feeling pretty cool stretching out at the start next to Walliser and Figini and the rest of the fastest 15 skiers in the world. At the beginning of the season, every one of them felt untouchable, and now I stood among them. On an ordinary day, that would have been enough. But I'd left my ordinary expectations at the Calgary Airport. I looked around at the other athletes, all hoping for the same thing. Why couldn't I be the one to get it?

This is the part where I was supposed to defy expectations with an out-of-body experience, to win a surprise medal in front of my family, my friends and my soon-to-be adoring fans and sponsors. This is where 90 seconds changes everything and secures my future. But this is a real story, and in real life things happen. Screwing up...and hanging in there, had become my specialty, and even though I wished I didn't have to show that off today, I did.

Three gates into the course, my outside ski slipped and turned fully sideways. I dumped most of my speed. At first I thought my ski had rattled off, but it was still there. Damn. There went my medal. But Jamie's old advice hammered in my head: "If you're going down, go down swinging." Instead of giving up, I flipped a switch and found hyper focus. I ran as tight a line as I could down the steep, then dropped into my lowest tuck, working every ripple on the flats. When I crossed the line and looked at the scoreboard I saw "4" next to my name. I should have been bummed, but three of the world's best racers were behind me despite my major blunder. I'd fought back, and I'd done well.

The crowd cheered and waved as enthusiastically as if I'd won, and I spotted my family in the bleachers, waving their American flags behind a homemade sign they had affixed to the bleachers. It had my name, a hammer and an arrow pointing down. I looked at the timing board and saw that I was less than a second away from Figini, who appeared to have a gold medal. Not bad. I had thought many times about what it might feel like to win a medal, had replayed it in my fantasies. I'd never gone through imagining what it would feel like to miss a medal. But now that I was here, I was surprised that it felt ok just to know I'd done my best.

In a few minutes, I'd have to leave this spot, exit through the two swinging gates and face a mob of reporters with their notepads and tape recorders and questions at the ready. But for now, I swept my head around to take one last look at the entire scene—the final few gates of the course leading through the finish banner with giant Olympic rings, the stadium full of people and just me on a huge white stage. I breathed it in and promised to hold part of that breath inside forever.

Epilogue:
The Best of the Worst

Here is the all-true ending to this story, as it played out for me and for my teammates.

A few minutes after my Super G run, Sigrid Wolf came down the course, skiing like she was possessed, like she had been saving up this run ever since Lech, when her victory had been snatched away over a safety pin. She crossed the line a full second ahead of Figini as if to say, "Take that, Switzerland!" The cowbells went silent.

The reporters surrounded me as I left the finish area and asked for comments about my run and the winners. One of them asked, "Do you think this is a turning point? Are things looking up for the US Ski Team?" Considering where we'd been, there was only one possible answer to that question.

"Absolutely."

What I told those reporters was right, sort of. We did get better and win medals but not there and certainly not in time for their deadlines. The best we did in Calgary was ninth place. My ninth place in the Super G. I can look back on it as being the best American skier at the Games, even though the press called it "The best the US could muster," and "The worst showing in 20 years." They didn't know what it took in terms of tenacity and sheer luck just to make it onto that team, let alone survive the season intact. And they had no clue of how many people might have had a better shot for gold but never got the chance. Our incredible shrinking family of athletes, coaches and reps did the best anybody could do with the situation that we had. It was a victory. They just don't give gold medals for those kinds of wins.

I went on to have World Cup success and to come close—as agonizingly close as an athlete is lucky to get—to achieving all I'd dreamed about. My teammates went on to win World Cups, World Championship and Olympic medals and, more importantly, to create leadership and breathing room for the next generation of American ski racers. One went on to be a World Champion many times over, and an Olympian, but not in skiing. Even the most severely injured recovered and returned to our team, if only long enough to prove that she could. In the end she put our experience into the best perspective. That year she had a lot of spare time to read—breaking your body into pieces does give you something at least—and along the way she read a quote about success that goes something like this:

"Success is not the act of never falling. It is the act of repeatedly getting up."

In the past four years, we had picked ourselves up and dusted ourselves off and believed in ourselves when nobody else did. Of the 30 of us who had been brought to the Shootout seven years earlier as "the future" of US Skiing, three survived to race in Calgary. The rest were injured or had been shoved out of the sport altogether.

As one teammate put it, "We may be the most successful team ever. Survivalhood is our badge. Just because our stories didn't have gold medal endings only means that our stories aren't done being written."